Did You Ever Think of Using These Everyday Household Objects as Games for Growth?
BEDSPREADS!   PILLOWS!
BROOM AND DUSTPAN!
A MESSY ROOM!   PAPER BAGS!
STAIRS!   CRAYONS!

Your toddler's second year is one of boundless energy and unlimited curiosity. Share in your child's tremendous eagerness to learn by playing these games of fun and discovery. You'll help increase your little one's:

- Ease with numbers
- Enjoyment of music
- Active imagination
- Motor skills and coordination
- Ability to share with others
  with . . .

GAMES TODDLERS PLAY

D1210948

Books by Julie Hagstrom

Games Babies Play & More Games Babies Play
   (with Joan Morrill)
Games Toddlers Play

Published by POCKET BOOKS

GAMES TODDLERS PLAY

JULIE HAGSTROM

Illustrated by
Christiane Stalland

PUBLISHED BY POCKET BOOKS NEW YORK

An *Original* publication of POCKET BOOKS

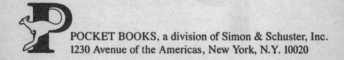

POCKET BOOKS, a division of Simon & Schuster, Inc.
1230 Avenue of the Americas, New York, N.Y. 10020

ISBN: 0-671-55506-5

First Pocket Books printing March, 1986

10 9 8 7 6 5 4 3 2 1

To Katie,
who continues to teach us
the meaning of
the word fun.

Acknowledgments

I would like to take this opportunity, because I never said it at the time, to thank Peggy Shima of Bear-Le-There Tots Gymnastics for sharing with me her ideas on creative play with kids.

And thank you, Matt McCue, for your original ideas and suggestions. (Hey, maybe you should write a book when you grow up!)

To Amy, who is never at a loss for a fresh (wild?) idea, I say thanks for everything.

And to busy Laura Champion and her even busier mom, Susie, I am forever grateful for their cooperation in our rapid-fire photo sessions.

Contents

Part II:
Fifteen to Eighteen Months
Active Toddler Games

Part III:
Eighteen to Twenty-One Months
Exploring Toddler Games

Part IV:
Twenty-One to Twenty-Four Months
Growing Toddler Games

GAMES
TODDLERS
PLAY

Introduction

After compiling over eighty games for the baby from birth to one year in *Games Babies Play* & *More Games Babies Play*, it only seemed fair that the toddler should have a set of games for learning, growing, and having fun, too! A baby's first year, even with its sleepless nights, emotional ups and downs, and family adjustments, is an exciting one indeed, but hold on to your hats, because it's in the second year that the fun really begins!

These are games that our daughter, Katie, played between her first and second birthdays. And, in all honesty, I must give credit where credit is due. The games are Katie's, not mine. I only happened to be watching and was lucky enough to be included. Oh, sure, sometimes I'd put in my two cents when I thought the game needed it, but Katie always started it! Let your child give you the gift of play. Explore her world through her eyes and discover the fun of toddlerhood the second time around—as a parent!* Because if there's anything Katie taught the rest of us that year, it was that having fun is what the toddler does best!

Your toddler's language development may be your

*Parents of boy toddlers, please adjust the *she*'s to *he*'s and *her*'s to *his*'s. After two daughters, it's a habit too hard to break.

biggest source of enjoyment during this year. Is there anything more thrilling than to hear that little voice calling "Mama! Mama!" as she toddles toward you all smiles? (Well, there *is* that first step, first haircut, and first real pair of underpants . . . as well as the first pony ride, first tooth, and that never-to-be-forgotten first birthday party. But who's counting?) And as soon as Katie let me know that she was ready, with her husky "All done!" and "Again!" (not to mention "No! No!"), we started playing all kinds of language games.

Games are also more fun now because the toddler is perfecting her motor skills. She doesn't lose interest in catching or chasing the ball like she used to because it's not as frustrating anymore.

However, speaking of frustration, the second year brings to light an age of independence! When twelve-month-old Katie began to refuse to hold my hand at crosswalks and shopping malls, my heart sank. I should have seen it coming; after all, Amy had been the same way. Somehow you think it won't happen to you (surely not *again*, anyway), but when that small hand stiffens and wriggles in yours, you'll know your time has come. Sometime during this year your toddler will want to feed herself, dress (or undress) herself, wash herself, you name it. One way to deal with this struggle for independence is to teach as many skills as you can through games. Sometimes interrupting a frustrated baby will only make her madder, but a game played later that shows how to open and close a cupboard without bumping the head will cheerfully get the point across.

But don't let all that "Me do it!" nonsense fool you! It's a topsy-turvy year in which your bold, independent toddler will have many moments of doubt and still need a lot of love and reassurance. Included here are plenty of games for those "clinging" days that not only distracted

Katie's fears or doubts but also gave me a chance to cuddle with a baby again. They grow so fast we often forget how little they really are.

Another big area of development is in social interaction. Finally your baby is looking beyond herself and wants to be included in anything anyone else is doing. It didn't matter what Amy was doing, Katie wanted to do it too. You can buy two of everything if you've an older sibling. That might help, but probably not! Katie not only wanted what Amy had, but she wanted to *be* where Amy was! She spent a great deal of time wedging herself in between Amy and the wall or even sitting directly on top of her. Katie would squeeze in next to Amy in the booster chair and stand beside her on the bathroom stool while Amy brushed her teeth. It can drive older siblings crazy, but, even though they may not admit it, they're flattered. So, many of the games are suitable for an older child or two. If special adaptations are necessary, you'll find them under the "Variations" section of the games. But, just as it was okay for us to play Candyland with Amy while Katie slept or played by herself, it was also okay for us to play a game with just Katie while Amy colored or napped. These games are here, too.

Even though these are our own family games, reflecting Katie's interests and development as a toddler, it's my hope that *Games Toddlers Play* will help you teach, get to know, and enjoy your toddler as much as we have ours. I've explained the origin of each game to give you an idea of what to listen for so that you can make up some of your own family favorites. Join us now in a turbulent, energy-filled year of games!

Part I

Twelve to Fifteen Months

Beginning Toddler Games

At about the time your baby takes her first steps, it will occur to you that this so-called baby isn't a baby anymore, but a toddler, teetering on the brink of real communication—not to mention quick getaways!

Looking forward to Katie's first birthday party, I expected to be struck suddenly with the realization that she and I had made it to that one-year milestone. But when the big day came I was too busy getting cake out of her hair and ice cream out of her dress to contemplate that first year of progress. But it's not something you see happen in one day anyway. Almost daily your baby surprises you with new words, bigger steps, and a better understanding of everything you say. Give plenty of encouragement and proud applause for these accomplishments—she's probably as surprised as you are at her new skills! Your enthusiasm and pride will rub off, giving her confidence in herself and the world around her.

And now that the world around your toddler is of more interest to her, be sure she sees it as a positive, okay place to grow up in. Her toys should be challenging but not frustrating, and outings should be planned with her more or less unpredictable needs in mind.

A good way to find easy activities is to let your toddler

choose them herself. At this age, Katie's favorite play periods weren't spent with her toys, but with everyday household objects. Taking the lids on and off kitchen pots and pans was a fun exercise, as was making music with wooden spoons. So watch your toddler to see what interests her. When she runs out of ideas, try a few of the following games for the beginning toddler.

1
Knock It Off!

Origin: We discovered this game in the bath one night. Katie's rubber duck was sitting on the edge of the tub, and when she bumped it off I joked, "Hey! Knock it off!" It got such a laugh out of her, I put it back up for a rerun. It makes a fun bath game, too—wet but fun!

Equipment: Any plastic bath or baby toys.

Position: Sit on the floor next to a low coffee table. Place your toddler across from you.

Procedure:
1. Set the toy in front of you and say, "Are you going to knock this over? I think you might knock this over!" Pull back, looking wary.
2. Your toddler will probably give you a blank look. So reach out and knock the toy off the table *toward yourself.*
3. When the toy is knocked off, gasp and pretend to be quite surprised.

Say, "Hey! Who did that? Who knocked it off?"

4. You're bound to get a chuckle with that!

5. Put the toy back into position, close enough for your baby to reach it, and say, "Boy, I wonder who will knock that toy off this time?"

6. If your toddler doesn't rise to the challenge, repeat step 2. If she does knock the toy down, gasp in surprise and say, "Hey! Hey you! Knock it off!"

7. Return the object to its original position and continue the game. Play as

Knock It Off!

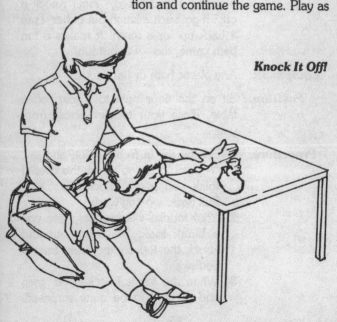

long as your toddler is interested. Even though Katie knew what would happen each time she knocked over the duck, she still burst out laughing at our surprised reactions.

Suggestions: Just a word to the wise: It's best to use plastic bath toys or blocks as opposed to cups (even unbreakable ones) or non-toy items. This will eliminate confusion over what is and what is not okay to knock over.

Also, stick to the dialogue suggested in the game, avoiding any commands such as "No, no! Don't knock it off!" Save that line for when you really need it!

Variations: Of course, when Amy was around, the girls took turns knocking the duck over, teaching Katie the valuable skill of waiting her turn.

2
Take That Baby!

Origin: Once, while sort of wrestling and sort of cuddling, Jerry (Katie's daddy) rolled Katie over as she lay on the rug. Then Amy got in on the act, and we discovered "Take That Baby!"

Equipment: No equipment is needed. However, you do need three players for this game. Mom and Dad can play, or include an older sibling.

Position: Lay your toddler on her back on a carpeted floor. The two other players kneel on either side of the toddler.

Procedure: 1. Lower your head and gently roll your baby over toward the other player. Say, "Hey! You take this baby!"

2. After rolling your toddler one full turn so she's in front of the other player, the second player lowers his head and says, "No! You take that baby!"

3. The second player gently rolls the toddler back to the first.

4. Watch for your toddler's reaction. Is she laughing? Good! Say to her, "What's so funny? Who are you laughing at? I don't want this silly baby . . . *you* take that baby!" And roll her back to your partner.

5. Continue a few more rounds, then say, "Oh, I'm just kidding! I guess this baby isn't so bad! I'll take this baby!" Pick her up, and give a big hug and kiss.

Suggestions: If your toddler is not interested in the game, spending most of her time struggling to get up and crawl away, try it again at a later date. Katie was never crazy about lying flat on her back, but she loved this game. We often played right after a diaper change since she was already in position.

Variations: An older brother or sister does quite well with this game. Amy enjoyed playing it with Katie, and after her turn Jerry and I could give Amy a few "Take That Baby!" rolls of her own!

3
Toddler Tag

Origin: Katie's hands were cold to the touch as I stepped out of the shower. Dodging those icy fingers gave us the idea for this game, which can be played either inside or outside.

Equipment: None.

Position: You and your toddler stand about three feet apart, facing each other.

Procedure:
1. Say to your child, "Come, try to touch Mommy—can't you touch Mommy?" Encourage her to take a step toward you and touch your leg.
2. But as your toddler approaches and reaches out to tag you, take a small step back. Say, "You didn't get me!"
3. Repeat step 1 and hop out of the way again, laughing and saying, "You didn't get me that time, either! Come on, Katie, try to tag Mommy!"

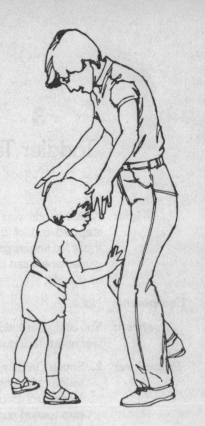

Toddler Tag

4. This time, let your toddler grab your leg. Say, "Oh! You got me!" (Big hug.)

Suggestions: If the toddler is reluctant to play "Toddler Tag," wait a month or so. Katie was fourteen months old when we played, and better able to understand verbal directions.

4

Leg Bounces

Origin: No toddler can resist that free-swinging leg, Katie included!

Equipment: None.

Position: Sit in a chair with your legs crossed. Straddle your toddler over the swinging ankle. Hold her hands or waist.

Procedure:
1. Gently bouncing your leg, say, "Look at Katie bouncing! Is that fun?"
2. Check to be sure she's enjoying herself.
3. Continue to bounce, explaining, "Up and down. We go *up* and *down*."
4. Imagine your bouncing leg is a horse and say, "Look at you ride this wild horse! Hang on tight!"
5. Take your toddler on an imaginary trip. "Where is this horse going? To the park?"
6. Make up more destinations for your

horse and rider, using words and places she's familiar with.

7. Bring your horse to a stop with a "Whoa!"

Suggestions: Something about one leg being crossed over the other tends to cut off all circulation in your bouncing horse! You'll have to pull the reins for periodic stops and stretches or stop the merry-go-round for more riders and additional dimes.

Variations: Your bouncing leg doesn't have to be a horse. If your toddler is familiar with merry-go-rounds, try that angle.

A quick song goes nicely with "Leg Bounces." "Over the river and through the woods," "Horsie, horsie, get on your way," or your own original jingle will make the ride more fun.

Leg Bounces

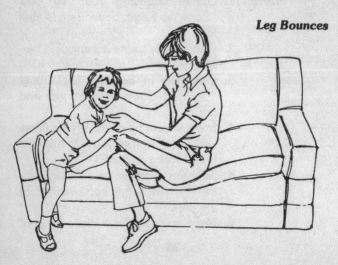

5
Monkey See, Monkey Do

Origin: Katie had a cup with pictures of Big Bird in three different positions. When I saw her trying to copy him with his hands over his eyes, I decided she was ready for this game.

Equipment: None.

Position: Sit on the floor facing your toddler.

Procedure:
1. Put your hands on your head and say, "Katie put *your* hands on *your* head!"
2. If she looks at you but doesn't copy you, lift her hands and place them on her head. Repeat, "Put your hands on your head."
3. Now switch to a different position (like "Put your hands on your tummy").
4. Continue this position until your toddler imitates it.
5. Go back to "Put your hands on your head."

6. Switch back and forth.

Suggestions: When you first start playing "Monkey See, Monkey Do," stick to working on two different positions. Introduce new ones after the first ones have been mastered.

Variations: Give the game a little more pizzazz by singing the commands.

An older child can have fun imitating the toddler or initiating some of the actions.

And you can think up some tricky ones for that older sibling, like "Put your nose on your knee!" We guarantee that will get a giggle from your toddler.

36

6
Keep on Truckin'

Origin: Toddlers and trucks just sort of gravitate to each other. You hardly need to teach them how to play, but here's a variation Katie especially liked.

Equipment: A selection of small toy cars or trucks.

Position: Sit on the floor with your toddler. Arrange the trucks in a line.

Procedure:
1. Picking out a truck or car, say, "I'm going to drive this one. Which truck do you want?" Help her select a truck or car.
2. "Rrrmmm, rrrmmm!" Drive your car along the floor.
3. Encourage your toddler to drive her car. "Come on, let's go!"
4. As soon as she is "rrrmmm, rrrmmm-ing" along the floor, say, "I'm going to the market. Are you? Let's drive to the market!"
5. Drive a few feet, then come to a screeching stop: "Errrk!"

6. Remind your toddler to stop too. "Hey, don't forget to stop at the red light!"

7. Now, drive your cars or trucks back home.

Suggestions: Taking a few small trucks or cars to a restaurant could save the day (or the dinner!).

Variations: Try racing your cars at an imaginary race track. "On your mark, get set . . ."

Older toddlers or siblings might enjoy pretending that certain spots are their house (under the chair), the market (behind the couch), and so forth.

If you have any trucks big enough for your toddler to sit on, she really can be in the driver's seat. But any ride toy can be a truck if you want it to be.

Keep On Truckin'

7

Animal Talk

Origin: Once, in the middle of a squirmy diaper change, I called out, "Katie! Katie!" It got her attention and she froze. But I knew it wouldn't last, so I followed up with "I know what a cow says! Do you?" It worked. I got her diaper changed by the third moo!

Equipment: None.

Position: Sit next to your toddler in her car seat or high chair, or hold your toddler in your arms or lap.

Procedure:
1. Begin a cheerful conversation with your toddler like this: "Katie? Do you know what a cow says?"
2. She waits for a hint.
3. "A cow says 'Moo, moo,' " you continue.
4. Encourage her to repeat the sound. "Can you say 'Moo,' Katie? Moo, moo!"

5. Any attempt at a sound should be rewarded with a kiss and "Good girl."

6. Go on to another animal, maybe a cat. "And do you know what the kitty-cat says, Katie?"

7. She waits . . . hoping for another hint!

8. "A cat says 'Meow, meow,'" you explain.

9. Again, encourage her to say the sound as you continue to name the animal.

10. It's a good idea to introduce only two or three animals at a time so as not to confuse your toddler.

Suggestions: "Animal Talk" comes in handy for the toddler who is recovering from a fall or is unhappy in a car seat.

It's a good idea to pick animals with which your toddler is familiar.

Animal Talk

Variations: This game is a natural with books. Either before or after introducing the game, find a book with animals—that's about all baby books have in them!—and show her a cow, cat, or dog. "See, Katie! This is a cow. This cow says 'Moo.' " This way she will recognize the animals' names as you play "Animal Talk" later without a book.

Of course, an older child will love showing off her expertise in "Animal Talk," but you can always throw in a few challenges, like "What does a hyena say?" or, better yet, "What does a bunny say?" That'll get them thinking (and quiet!) for a minute!

8

This Little Piggy

Origin: Who can resist this classic while trying to slip a sock over five wiggly toes? It hardly needs to be taught, but just as a reminder, here's how it goes.

Equipment: Toes!

Position: Sit with your toddler on your lap, or have her sit on a chair to have her shoes put on.

Procedure:
1. Grasping the toddler's big toe between your thumb and forefinger, wiggle it back and forth and chant, "This little piggy went to market."
2. Move on to the next toe, giving it a good squeeze, and say, "This little piggy stayed home."
3. Grab the next toe and say, "This little piggy ate roast beef" ("pea soup" for vegetarians).
4. Next toe: "This little piggy had none." Wail.

5. Baby toe: "And this little piggy went 'Wee, wee, wee,' all the way home!" Wiggle the toe rapidly back and forth.

6. Stop for a hug break before going on to the other foot.

Suggestions: You'd be surprised how many older kids love to have their piggies go to market!

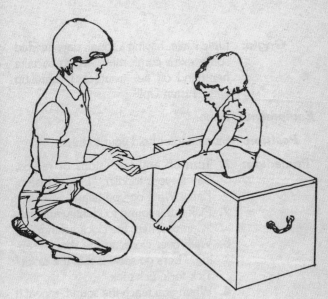

This Little Piggy

9
Listen Up!

Origin: Little Katie, having a rough day, needed some extra comforting. Trying to take her mind off her troubles, I came up with "Listen Up!"

Equipment: None.

Position: Sit next to or hold your toddler.

Procedure:
1. Turn off any televisions or radios. Say to your toddler, "Listen! Listen, Katie! What do you hear?"
2. Pick out a sound to identify and say, "Can you hear the clock ticking?"
3. Walk over closer to the sound, saying, "Let's go see—is that the clock? Tick tock, tick tock."
4. When you reach the sound, repeat it ("Tick tock, tick tock") and name the sound maker.
5. Stop talking, stand very still, holding your toddler, and say, "What else do you hear?"

6. If she should point in a direction or indicate in some way that something interests her, then follow that lead. Otherwise, choose another sound (like the refrigerator) to track down: "Hear the humming, Katie? Hmm, hmm. What's that sound?"

7. Continue through a few more sounds. She may lose interest after that anyway.

Listen Up!

Suggestions: You need a quiet house to play this game in because you are trying to make your baby aware of all the little sounds around her. It's a good calming game before a nap or when your toddler seems to need some extra holding or soothing.

Variations: Often, a sound heard inside the house will lead you outside in tracking it down. When this happens, a whole new world of sounds opens up. Birds, cars, trucks, kids playing, lawnmowers, or airplanes can all be heard if you listen carefully. Obviously, you can't track down these noise makers, but you can point to many of them.

This is a great game for older brothers or sisters. They will enjoy the challenge of listening for a barking dog or a crying baby.

A trip to the beach or the mountains opens up a whole new range of sounds, too.

10
Body Language

Origin: Since "eye" was one of the first words Katie said, it just seemed logical to follow it up with "nose," "ears," and "mouth"!

Equipment: None.

Position: Any.

Procedure:
1. Start by asking, "Do you know where Mommy's eyes are?" Now point to your eyes, saying, "That's right! Here are my eyes."
2. Ask, "Where are your eyes, Katie?"
3. Help her indicate her eyes.
4. Encourage her to say "eye" as she points to either your or her eyes.
5. Move along to the nose. "Where is your nose? Is *that* [touching the nose] your nose?"
6. "Where is Mommy's nose?"
7. "Can you say 'nose'?"
8. Remember, this is a game, not a lesson, so keep it fun! Say, "Hey, can

I *honk* your nose?" Give her nose a little squeeze while simultaneously making a honking noise. This ought to get a laugh!

9. Find and label each other's ears, mouths, hair, and chins.

Suggestions: This is an excellent restaurant or car game.

Don't add too many new parts until your toddler is familiar with the first ones.

Variations: Play "Body Language" with a doll or stuffed animal.

An older toddler will want to know what each part of the body does. "These are your eyes. They can blink."

When your toddler has mastered the parts of the head, move on down to her hands, tummy, and feet.

11

Eat, Drink, and Be Merry

Origin: This learning game was developed in hopes of teaching Katie to feed herself . . . successfully!

Equipment: One child-size and one regular-size cup, spoon, and bowl. Some cereal and juice.

Position: Place your toddler in her high chair and put a small amount of juice, milk, or water in her cup. The best cereal for beginning eaters is either oatmeal or soggy cereal (pour milk, let sit a minute, then pour off excess milk).

Put her bowl in front of her, spoon facing the right hand.

Give yourself some juice and cereal in your bowl and cup.

Procedure: 1. Start with the cup. "Do you have a cup like Mommy? We both have cups of juice!"

2. Demonstrate the two-hands method of holding the cup. Position her hands around her cup.

3. The key to safe drinking is in *slowly* lifting the cup and *slowly* tipping the juice into the mouth. So explain, "You don't want to scare your juice! Oh no! It will jump out! Go slowly." Lift your cup slowly to your mouth in demonstration.

4. Now it's her turn. Help her *slowly* lift the cup to her mouth.

Eat, Drink, and Be Merry

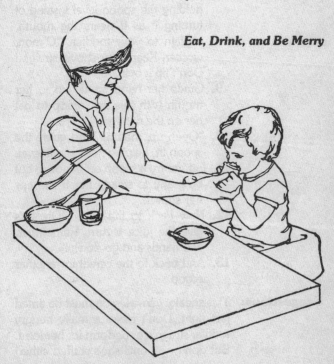

5. Show her how she should tip the juice into her mouth. Say, "Just a little at a time. Don't rush in, juice!"

6. With your hand hovering close by, let her try a sip on her own.

7. Now for the cereal. Unless your toddler shows a preference, encourage her to use her right hand. Guiding her hand over the spoon handle, scoop up some cereal.

8. Since the trick to clean eating is in holding the spoon level instead of turning it as it nears the mouth, explain to your toddler, "C'mon, worker! Keep your shovel straight! Don't tip it over."

9. Guide her hand gently up to her mouth with this first scoop to get her on the right track.

10. "Open up, mouth!" and guide the spoon in, helping her keep it level.

11. Let her try a scoop on her own, but be ready to steady her if she tips her shovel.

12. Now back to the juice. "Oh, let's give the juice a turn. Remember, two hands and go slowly!"

13. And back to the cereal for another scoop.

Suggestions: This sneaky game/lesson must be timed just right. Don't make a really hungry toddler struggle or perform for her food. But don't wait until she's stuffed either!

Somewhere halfway through the meal is best.

There are all kinds of spoons for the beginning eater on the market, but we found that the short-handled teaspoons from my grandmother's silver set worked best.

Variations: "Eat, Drink, and Be Merry" can be played in a pretend tea party set up with no real food or drink. If you've got a reluctant eater (or a really sloppy one), this may get her thinking.

12

Do You Want to Know a Secret?

Origin: I made up this self-esteem game to give Katie some good feelings about herself and the world around her.

Equipment: None.

Position: Hold your toddler close, either on your lap or in your arms. A rocking chair is nice.

Procedure:
1. Whisper in her ear, "Listen! Do you want to know a secret?"
2. Your toddler might giggle at the ticklish feeling in her ear.
3. Continue whispering, "Here's my secret. It's a secret about Katie! You are a *good* girl."
4. Probably more giggles.
5. Switch to the other ear. "Oh! I have another secret . . . listen!"
6. Pause for dramatic effect.

7. Whisper, "I love you!" and give a big hug!

8. Continue whispering loving positive messages as long as the receiver is having a good time.

Suggestions: Anything your toddler has done especially well that day could be used as the secret. "Katie shared her toys" and "Katie picked up her blocks" make good secrets.

Do You Want to Know a Secret?

Mentioning other members of the family will give your toddler something to think about. "Daddy loves Katie" is important for her to hear, too!

Variations: Older siblings especially like and need to be told special secrets. And they can also be encouraged to give secrets to the little toddler.

An older toddler might like to try giving you a secret, although it may lose something—like the meaning—in the translation.

13
Where's the Water?

Origin: Once, in an attempt to divert Katie's attention from the hose with which I was watering our new grass, I directed her to another faucet, letting her play in its slow drips. Delighted with the idea, she ran in search of other such sources of water.

Equipment: None.

Position: Any.

Procedure:
1. Hold your toddler up to the kitchen sink and turn on the faucet. Let her run her hands under the water while you explain, "Water! We found water in the sink!"
2. Ask, "Where else is there water? Can we find more water?"
3. If she wants to show you another source, follow along. Otherwise, lead her into the bathroom and turn on the shower or tub.

4. Say, "Look! Here's some more water! Feel that cold water!"

5. Continue your search for water, either following your toddler's lead or vice versa. Be sure to hit all the obvious sources like sinks, tubs, and showers, as well as those not-so-obvious places like the washing machine and dishwasher.

6. Now go outside. Ask, "Is there any water outside? Where is the water outside?"

7. Again, lead or be led to outside sources such as hoses, faucets, and sprinklers.

8. If you make it to the outside sources, especially the hose, the game will

more than likely end there. One game's end is another game's beginning!

Suggestions: Be sure to act surprised with each new discovery. Your toddler will begin to anticipate your reaction with as much delight as the discovery of the water. A look of surprise and a startled "Oh!" will soon bring on gales of laughter.

Variations: You can talk about hot and cold water at many locations as well as how water feels, sounds, and tastes. You might even want to explain what the water at various taps is used for. "This water washes our dishes" or "this water fills the bathtub," for example.

Then there's finding water as is, in the dog's water bowl, for example, the tea kettle, goldfish bowl, or gutter. And, again, if you get to the gutter, it's all over!

14

Whose Shoes?

Origin: What is it about shoes that fascinates the toddler? If the closet doors were left open, Katie couldn't get in there fast enough to drag out every shoe she could find.

Equipment: Shoes, preferably still in the closet.

Position: Any.

Procedure:
1. Ask, "Where are Mommy's shoes? Can you find Mommy's shoes?"
2. Follow her as she leads you to the closet.
3. When the closet door opens to reveal the shoes, exclaim, "Oh, my! Look at all those shoes! Are those *Mommy's* shoes?" Agree with her that they are indeed Mommy's shoes.
4. Suggest, "Let's put all Mommy's shoes in a row."

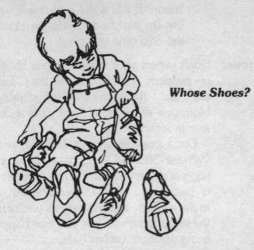

Whose Shoes?

5. Help her get started on this project if she seems unsure about what to do.
6. When all the shoes are lined up, say, "There! All Mommy's shoes are in a row!"
7. Then ask, "Where are Daddy's shoes?"
8. Repeat steps 3 through 6 with Daddy's shoes.
9. If you have the time and she has the interest, continue to find and line up the different shoes of each family member, including her own.
10. Putting the shoes away could go either way. Your toddler may enjoy arranging shoes back in closets, or she may object to disturbing her

lineup! If this is the case, have her
line up the shoes *inside* the closet
the next time you play!

Suggestions: Don't expect your toddler to pair shoes
up properly. That will come later. Just
the fact that she's distinguishing
Mommy's shoes from Daddy's is a big
step in sorting.

Once your toddler is familiar with
"Whose Shoes?" it's a great game to
suggest when you need a few moments
of peace and quiet to get dressed or
make a phone call. As long as you're in
the same room with her, she'll be happy
lining up shoes on her own.

Variations: Your toddler will undoubtedly come up
with all sorts of ways to vary "Whose
Shoes?" Katie enjoyed the obvious—
trying on each shoe as well as pushing
them along the carpet as though they
were boats.

15
Stack and Whack!

Origin: What toddler can resist knocking over a stack of blocks piled ten high? As destructive as it may first appear, I'm sure it all has to do with learning cause and effect and, of course, the wonderful sound made when blocks crash onto the kitchen floor. Since Katie learned to crawl backwards before she could go forward and to undress before she could dress, it came as no surprise to us that she'd rather knock it down than stack it up!

Equipment: Wooden or plastic blocks, or any type of plastic containers.

Position: Sit on the floor across from your toddler with the blocks between you.

Procedure:
1. Demonstrate the art of block stacking by placing four or five blocks on top of each other in a kind of tower.
2. Say, "Look how I *stack* the blocks!"

3. Now demonstrate the *whack* half of the game by gently knocking the tower over and saying, "Whack! Down go the blocks!"

4. This should induce a smile, if not a chuckle.

5. Restack the blocks for your toddler, higher this time, and say, "Do you want to *whack* down the blocks?" (Does a bear sleep in the woods?)

Stack and Whack!

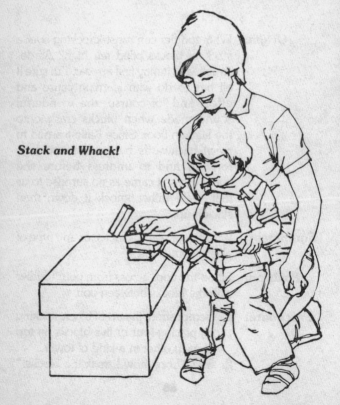

6. Applaud your toddler after her successful whack.

7. Restack the blocks, even higher this time, and repeat steps 5 and 6.

8. By now she's got the hang of the game, and you can continue as above or try one of the variations below.

Suggestions: Play "Stack and Whack" on a hard surface for more dramatic sound effects.

Don't use food cans; they can come crashing down on small toes and fingers.

Variations: Let your toddler try the stacking, and *you* do the whacking.

Count the blocks as you stack them to introduce this learning skill.

Use different parts of the body to whack the blocks with. The nose, foot, knee, and elbow all work as good whackers!

An older sibling will enjoy this game and could even be the one to introduce it.

16
Pillow Talk

Origin: Not unlike Goldilocks trying out beds and chairs, Katie used to enjoy trying out pillows. It's hard to say what she really had in mind with her lineup of pillows, but I interpreted the game as follows.

Equipment: An assortment of bed pillows and/or cushions.

Position: Line the pillows up on the floor and then sit at one end of the row with your toddler.

Procedure: 1. Say, "Look at all these pillows! Some are big, some are small."
2. Rest your head on the first pillow and say, "Oh, this pillow is too hard!" (or soft, or big, or whatever is appropriate for that pillow).
3. Move over to the next pillow, again resting your head there for a mo-

ment before announcing that it's too flat or too bumpy, and so on.

4. Continue through the line of pillows until you think your toddler has caught on to the game.

5. Suggest, "Now *you* try these pillows. Do you like this first pillow?"

6. Since your toddler probably won't be able to clearly communicate the various pillows' faults, go ahead and fill in the blanks for her, saying, "Oh, is it too little?" And then, "Oh well! Try the next one!"

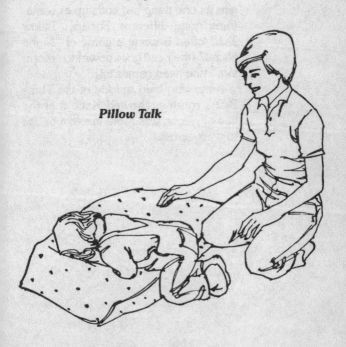

Pillow Talk

7. Continue "Pillow Talk" until your toddler loses interest.

Suggestions: Once you've played "Pillow Talk" a few times, let your toddler be the one who sets up the pillows.

Katie used to speed through the line of pillows at such a rate that her head barely grazed their surfaces. If this should happen to you, space the pillows out so she can't get to the next one so quickly.

Variations: This is the kind of game that often begins as one thing but ends up as something quite different. For us, "Pillow Talk" often became a game of "Night! Night!" (the head goes down) to "Morning!" (the head comes up).

Amy, who tired quickly of the Three Bears routine, showed Katie that the line of pillows was more fun as a bridge to walk across.

17
Brushing Up

Origin: Katie adored Amy's Spiderman tooth-brush holder, and whenever she could maneuver the bathroom stool into the right position she'd busy herself playing with the assortment of brushes it held.

Equipment: Toothbrush (several will make the game more fun), mirror, and toothpaste (optional).

Position: Stand your toddler on a stool so she can see herself in the mirror. Position yourself beside her.

Procedure:
1. Point to the various toothbrushes and say, "Look at these tooth-brushes! Do you want to try one?"
2. Let her select a brush. Because they never miss a trick, she'll undoubtedly know what to do with it.
3. Remind her what the brush is for: "Scrub your teeth (what, all four?) so they're nice and clean."

4. Then suggest, "Do you want to try *this* toothbrush?" indicating another brush on the counter.

5. She probably will, so repeat steps 2 and 3 with this brush.

6. Point to the mirror and say, "Look! There you are brushing your teeth!" And then, "Let's see how clean your teeth are now." Encourage your toddler to grin widely into the mirror.

7. Try putting a dab of toothpaste on her brush. If she doesn't like it, rinse it off.

8. Move on to another brush if your toddler is still interested in the game.

Suggestions: Be sure to get the brush wet before she begins brushing.

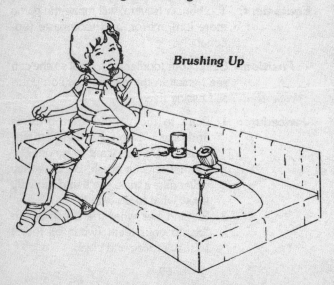

Brushing Up

Explain that the toothbrush is only for teeth, not hair or floors or pets, or you'll be buying them every week!

This is a great give-me-five-minutes-to-unload-the-dishwasher game!

Variations: The toothbrush holder itself can make a great game. Katie delighted in putting brushes in and out of their little slots.

When brushing, identify the tongue, gums, and roof of the mouth, just for fun.

18
Keeper of the Keys

Origin: Like every other toddler in the world, Katie found a bunch of keys to be a great source of amusement. Somehow sensing their importance in the adult world, Katie took her job as "Keeper of the Keys" very seriously.

Equipment: A set of old keys, the more the better.

Position: Any.

Procedure:
1. Handing your toddler her own set of keys, say, "Now you have keys like Mommy and Daddy!"
2. Now point to a door, drawer, or cupboard and exclaim, "Oh! I need to open this cupboard, but it's locked!"
3. Ask your toddler to use her keys to unlock the cupboard.
4. If she doesn't understand what's expected of her, show her how to pretend to unlock the cupboard by turning the key in an imaginary lock.

5. After she unlocks the cupboard, clap your hands and say, "Oh, thank you! Now I can open my cupboard!"

6. Choose another drawer, door, or cupboard, and repeat steps 3 through 5.

7. Walk through the house looking for

things that open and close so your
toddler can unlock them for you.
Jewelry boxes, medicine cabinets,
and windows can all be unlocked.

8. Once you've exhausted all lockable
   sources, find a good place for your
   toddler to keep her keys. If you usually keep yours in a purse, then find
   a small purse for your toddler's keys.
   If you hang them on a hook, then
   arrange a key hook for her that she
   can reach.

Suggestions: Be sure to ham it up when you come to
a door or cupboard you want your tod-
dler to unlock. Tug on it and make it
really look locked!

Variations: Keys also make things go. Your young
"Keeper of the Keys" could also pretend
to turn on the vacuum cleaner, dishwasher, or television.

An older sibling will enjoy playing
with a key and padlock. Many types of
locks and keys can be found at the
hardware store, and even your toddler
will be able to manage some.

Part II

Fifteen to Eighteen Months

Active Toddler Games

Well, I have some good news and some bad news. The good news is that your fifteen-month-old is soon to become a very confident walker, then runner, then climber! The bad news is that you're going to have trouble catching her . . . and keeping her. Fifteen months begins an explosion of activity and exploration. Just try to keep a squirming toddler in a stroller! Amy's nonstroller stage peeked at Christmastime, and it was slow going at the mall with Amy pushing the stroller in circles, bumping into fellow shoppers' heels. That was the year I discovered the Sears catalog.

Dealing with a determined fifteen-month-old can be frustrating and discouraging, but be patient; it will pass. Once the thrill of walking by herself wears off, your toddler will allow you to push her in the stroller again. But for the time being, avoid situations you know will be difficult for her to handle. Even going for a walk can become a source of conflict if your toddler stops at every sprinkler head, stepping stone, and mailbox when you had a faster pace or specific destination in mind. While walks that went no further than the corner manhole used to drive my husband crazy, Grandma knew better than to rush a toddler. "What's the hurry?" Ah, to be a grandparent and enjoy the luxury of patience!

But your toddler probably isn't as determined or as independent as she's led you to believe. She still likes you in sight while she plays, watching for your approval and listening for your comments. So let her know you're there and that you think she's great.

And when she wants more from you than a few kind words, take some time out to play the following games with your active toddler.

19
Bzzt! Bleep!

Origin: Picture this: I'm peacefully reading my book when Katie flops on my legs. I let out a surprised "Bleep!" Katie laughs, and the fun begins.

Equipment: None.

Position: Any.

Procedure: 1. The next time your toddler gives you an unexpected poke or flop, respond with your own unexpected "Bzzt!"

2. She'll probably laugh and poke or touch you again, to which you repeat, "Bzzt!"

3. By now she has figured out that this is a game and will continue to push the right buttons for your "Bzzt!" response.

4. Now change the reaction to her push or touch. Instead of a "Bzzt!" give her a "Bleep!" and she'll really go to pieces!

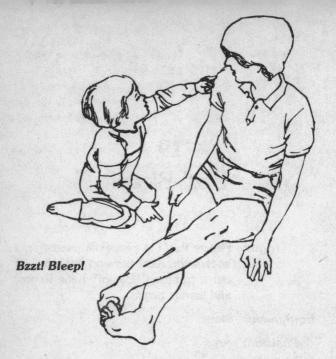

Bzzt! Bleep!

5. Continue "Bleeping" at the appropriate moments until you've had enough.

6. End up the game with a big hug and kiss, saying, "What a silly game! You made me Bzzt! and Bleep!"

Suggestions: Along with the sound effects, be sure to make a surprised or funny face. Try changing the tone of your "Bzzts" and "Bleeps," too.

If you can't wait for your partner to initiate the action, ask her to touch your knee or sit on your leg.

Variations: Reverse the game, telling her to "Bzzt!" when you touch her.

Play dumb, not responding at all until she pokes you somewhere new (on the leg instead of the arm, for example). This will make her think twice!

Older siblings enjoy being both the "Bleepee" and the "Bleeper."

20
It's in the Bag

Origin: Having an older sibling can come in handy. Amy, age four, gave us the idea of hiding in the bag, and Katie and I modified it to suit toddlers.

Equipment: Large grocery bag.

Position: Place the bag over your own head. Sit, stand, or kneel in front of your toddler.

Procedure:
1. Say, "Oh! Where's Mommy? Is she under the bed?"
2. Your toddler will probably just stand there, fascinated.
3. Guess some other possible places where you could be hiding that would be familiar to your toddler. "Is Mommy in the cupboard? Under the television?"
4. Finally, pull off the bag, saying, "Here she is!"
5. Repeat steps 1 through 4, guessing different hiding places.

6. Ask your toddler if *she* would like to hide in the bag.

7. Slowly place the bag over her head and say, "Where's Katie? Behind the couch?"

8. Quickly guess a few more places if she hasn't pulled the bag off yet.

9. Then gently pull the bag off, exclaiming, "Here she is! I found Katie!"

10. Let her hide under the bag again if she enjoyed it, or hide yourself again.

It's in the Bag

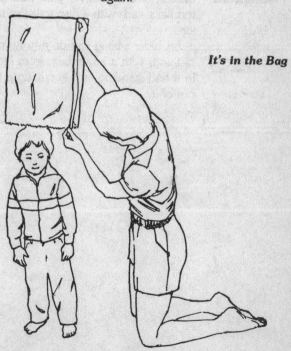

11. End the game by saying, "Well, we were in the bag all along, weren't we? Hiding in the bag!"

Suggestions: If your toddler doesn't feel comfortable with the bag over her head, just skip that part and try again in a few weeks.

Some toddlers like the bag pulled off with a dramatic flare, and some think it's funny if you feel the outside of the bag, saying, "What could this be? This feels like a nose!"

Variations: Instead of a bag, cover your (and your toddler's) face with a dish towel or napkin.

An older sibling can do any number of things with a paper bag, from hiding in it and standing in it to cutting a face out of it.

21
Left, Right!
Left, Right!

Origin: Living in a house with stairs, we felt it safer for toddler Katie to learn how to crawl backwards down them than always to rely on the guard gate that could be left ajar.

Equipment: A set of stairs ranging anywhere from two to ten. A small stepstool or child's indoor slide with a ladder can also be used.

Position: Stand, sit, or kneel with your toddler at the top of the stairs.

Procedure: Most toddlers will try crawling down stairs head first. But even after a first disastrous step, ending in a head-over-heels roll, instinct does not take over and solve the mystery of getting down once you're up. It's a skill that must be taught.

85

1. Begin by saying, "Uh-oh! Here are the stairs! How are you going to get down?"

2. As soon as she tries to crawl forward, say, "Nope! Not that way. Turn around and go *backwards.*"

3. If she doesn't do it herself, turn her so she's in position to crawl backwards down the stairs.

4. Now encourage her—"There! Now right *leg* down, right *hand* down!"—and help her along.

Left, Right! Left, Right!

5. Repeat for the next step and chant, "Leg down, hand down. Left, right! Left, right!" while you help.

6. Once you reach the bottom, let her scamper back up again and start all over.

Suggestions: Even if you don't have stairs in your house, getting down them is a real all-purpose skill to have mastered. How many times has your excited toddler stepped right off the edge of a small doorstep or patio deck, taking a hard fall? When she knows how to maneuver stairs, you'll find your toddler backing out of chairs, down steps, and over other obstacles with a lot fewer falls.

Variations: Has your toddler ever climbed up the high ladder on the park slide only to change her mind about sliding down? It happens a lot and is as good an opportunity as any to teach "Left, Right! Left, Right!"

Going up the stairs is not included in "Left, Right! Left, Right!" and can be taught with the same procedure as going down, but most toddlers figure out how to go up all on their own.

22

One, Two, Three . . . Jump!

Origin: Seeing Katie's pathetic attempt at a jump, I decided to give her some help.

Equipment: A pillow or couch cushion.

Position: Stand your toddler on top of a pillow. Sit in front of her.

Procedure:
1. Say, "Here we go! Are you ready to jump?" Hold her hands and help her jump up and down on top of the pillow.
2. Still holding her hands, say, "One, two, three . . . jump!" And on "jump," lift her up off the pillow and onto the carpet.
3. Big hug.
4. Position the toddler on the pillow again and see if she'll jump on her own. If she wants to hold hands, by all means do so.

One, Two, Three . . . Jump!

5. Count off, "One, two, three . . . jump!" This time, wait for her to indicate to you whether or not she needs help. She may try it on her own.

6. Keep at it until one of you tires.

Suggestions: If your toddler is having difficulty getting both feet off the ground at once (not an easy task), let her just bend her knees as you count "One, two, three . . ."

The jump may also be a kind of flop or crawl, but it's the right idea.

Variations: When jumping from one pillow becomes too easy, add a pillow to the jumping platform.

A daring toddler may want to jump from the couch into her parents' arms. We found that teaching Katie (quite the daring toddler) only to jump after her partner counted "One, two, three . . ." avoided falls into midair or unexpected leaps into our laps. So be consistent in your countdown!

23
In and Out

Origin: Katie made up this game while camping, and when it was time for me to fix dinner all available pots were filled with pine cones and dusty rocks!

Equipment: Two beach buckets or unbreakable bowls. A handful of blocks, smooth rocks, or shells.

Position: Put all the rocks into one bucket. Place this and the empty bucket in front of your toddler.

Procedure:
1. Draw your toddler's attention to the full bucket. Say, "Oh, look at this bucket of pretty rocks."
2. Put one of the rocks into the empty bucket. Ask, "Should we take the rocks *out* of this bucket and put them *in* this one?"
3. She may want them left in their original bucket. If so, let her figure out what she wants to do.

4. Otherwise, encourage her to help you transfer the rocks. Repeat, "We are taking the rocks out of this bucket and putting them in here!"

5. When all the rocks have been transferred, she may want to take them out again, or pour them out or, and this is popular, carry the bucket around with her.

Suggestions: Adapt this game to any situation, using whatever's available.

Stress the words *in* and *out*. She might as well learn as she plays!

Variations: It might be interesting simply to give your toddler the materials for the game and let her create her own version of "In

In and Out

and Out." Watch closely. You may learn something about your toddler and how she plays.

Did your toddler crawl backwards before going forward? Can she take her clothes off but not put them on? Then she'll probably enjoy taking the rocks *out* of buckets before she wants to put things *in* the bucket. If you have dresser drawers to clean out or cupboards to straighten, let your little toddler help pull the contents *out* of drawers or cupboards. She may lose interest as you place things *in* neatly, but it's as good a beginning to "picking up" as creeping backwards is to crawling forward!

24
Bed Bugs

Origin: It never failed that each morning, just as I was making my bed, Katie would toddle in and want to hide under the bedspread as I shook it out over the bed.

Equipment: A bedspread ready to be rumpled. A large quilt or blanket could also be used.

Position: Your toddler scrambles up on the unmade bed, and you hold the bedspread/blanket/quilt.

Procedure:
1. Shake the bedspread or quilt out over your toddler and say, "There! Now my bed is made, nice and neat!"
2. Pretending surprise, you say, "Oh! My goodness! What is this big lump under here?"
3. Feel on top of the covers. "Hey, this feels like a head!"
4. Continue patting the lump and finding various parts of her body. "Here's the legs . . . and bottom!"

Bed Bugs

5. Finally, you come to the conclusion that there's somebody under your spread. "Hey! Who's under there? Who is this bed bug?"

6. Dramatically pulling back the spread, exclaim, "Oh, it's Katie!"

7. If she enjoyed it at all, she'll ask for a repeat. As Katie would say, "Do dat adin!" So repeat steps 1 through 7.

8. Now make your bed.

Suggestions: Repeat the game as many times as the two of you want, but when you've had enough be sure to give fair warning before the last round. It's easier to accept the end of a game if you can see it coming.

Some toddlers don't feel comfortable being totally covered with a spread. Try flapping the spread up and down over her until she feels safe enough to let it rest on her for a moment.

Variations: "Bed Bugs" originated on a bed but can just as easily be played on the floor with a sheet, blanket, or towel.

After feeling the head, legs, arms, and so on, make a series of wrong guesses about what the bed bug is. An elephant? A car? And, finally, pull the cover off to find "Oh! It's only Katie!"

Let an older child play and the toddler crawl or sit on the covered sibling. Katie enjoyed clambering over hidden Amy, saying, "This a head? This a foot?"

"Bed Bugs" can be reversed so that the parent is the bed bug and the toddler guesses who's there. Begin by sticking just your legs under a blanket, wiggling them, and saying "Oh, look! What's under the blanket?"

25

Soap Box Derby

Origin: After unpacking from a camping trip, Amy and Katie squeezed into the empty boxes strewn on the kitchen floor. It was Katie's idea to make them go "Beep, beep," but it was Amy's idea to make them crash!

Equipment: Cardboard boxes (as many boxes as players) big enough for a toddler or sibling to sit in.

Position: Each toddler sits in a box. What child can resist the privacy and security of her own cardboard box?

Procedure:
1. Amy started this one by saying, "Hey, Katie! I'll race you! Vrrrum, vrrrum," and she would rock her box back and forth.
2. Katie, not to be outdone, said, "Beep, beep," as she pushed on a pretend horn.
3. A fifteen- to eighteen-month-old may have some difficulty rocking her

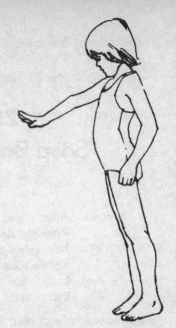

box or making it scoot anywhere, but she'll probably be happy just to sway back and forth.

4. "Red light!" called Amy as she screeched to a stop. Katie copied.

5. "Green light!" What else? And the drivers were rocking and swaying down the road again!

6. Amy finally rocked her way over to where Katie was driving in place. As Amy's car lightly bumped Katie's, Amy cried, "Oh no! A car crash!" And she tipped herself over. This was Katie's favorite part of the game, and Amy enjoyed hamming it up.

Suggestions: If you don't have any siblings or toddler friends to drive with, kneel next to your toddler's car as you go through the red light, green light, stop-and-go routine.

Variations: Using marking pens or crayons, decorate the cars with headlights, steering wheels, horns, and wheels.

Have a race, pretending the cars are rounding the curve, coming down the home stretch, and crossing the finish line.

26
Turnabout's Fair Play!

Origin: As soon as your toddler can crawl, and even as soon as she can grab, she will want a piece of the action! No matter what Katie had, she wanted the toy Amy was playing with. While there's a tendency to "let the baby have it," you're not doing her any favor by giving in to unfair demands. We made up a learning game to teach this hard lesson in life, hoping it would carry over into her day-to-day play.

Equipment: Any two toys.

Position: Sit comfortably beside your toddler.

Procedure:
1. Begin by saying, "It's your turn for the truck" (or whatever she's playing with). Continue, "It's *not* my turn. I have the blocks" (or whatever).
2. Play a few moments with your respective toys.
3. Then say, "Now it's Mommy's turn for the truck. Katie had a turn, and

Turnabout's Fair Play

now Mommy gets a turn. (It's best not to ask, "May I have a turn?" because chances are she'll say "No!")

4. Pick up her toy and exchange it for yours. Say, "You can play with the blocks, and I can play with the truck!"
5. Give her a big hug and say, "You're such a good girl at taking turns!"
6. Let her enjoy the blocks for a while before trading again.

Suggestions: Stick to one word, like "turn," whenever you refer to sharing or trading toys.

This skill is difficult enough to learn without the confusion of different terms.

Always exchange one toy for another when taking turns. Your toddler is too young to wait empty-handed.

Variations: After she's played "Turnabout's Fair Play" with you a few times, the idea of sharing should be encouraged during her daily play with other children. A quick reminder of "Remember how we take turns when we play?" will make this easier.

Play "Turnabout's Fair Play" at the park while taking turns on the slide or swing.

27
Hello, Goodbye!

Origin: Katie started this by saying "Goodbye!" every time I said "Hello!" I'm sure your toddler will think it's as hilarious as Katie did.

Equipment: None.

Position: Anywhere there's a door.

Procedure:
1. You can start by peeking around the door at your toddler and saying, "Hello!"
2. Then quickly say, "Oh! Goodbye!" and pull yourself out of sight.
3. Wait a few seconds and hope she comes looking for you.
4. If she doesn't, repeat steps 1 and 2.
5. When she does peek around the door, say, "Hello!"
6. Encourage her to join the fun. "Can you say 'Hello!' to Mommy?"
7. Getting her to take the more active part now, say, "Now can you tell me 'Goodbye!'?"

Hello, Goodbye!

8. After a few trials of steps 5 and 6, she'll catch on to peeking around the door to say "Hello!" and pulling out of sight to say "Goodbye!"

Suggestions: Respond to her with expression in your face and voice. Children love a big reaction, especially Katie, who thought our surprised faces were hilarious.

Variations: We played "Hello, Goodbye!" in the swing. Standing in front of the swing, I would say, "Hello!" as Katie glided toward me and "Goodbye!" as I gave her a push and she swung away.

28

Clean-Up Countdown

Origin: Along about fifteen months old, we began expecting Katie to help pick up her toys. But since we didn't want to end a happy play period in a negative way, we developed this game.

Equipment: A messy room. We'll use blocks as the example.

Position: Any.

Procedure:
1. Begin with yourself: "I'm picking up one block." Put your block away.
2. Now hand your toddler a block and say, "Katie has one block to put away." Indicate where she should put her block.
3. This time, you put two blocks away and hand your toddler two to put away.
4. Again, count the blocks out loud to her. "Two for you, two for me. Put them away!"

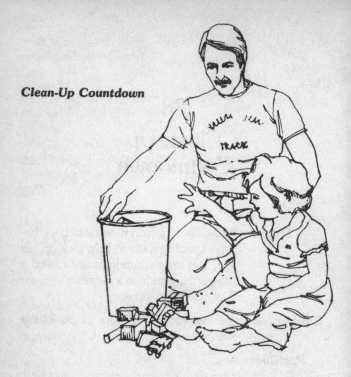

5. If she's reluctant to help, encourage her verbally, and either bring the block container to her or gently lead her to where they should go.
6. Give her a pat on the back and a "good girl" when she finally gets a block put away.
7. Continue counting, "Now I have three blocks! Can you pick up three?" or switch to a color. "I have a red block! What color do you want to put away?"

8. When the job is done, remark to your toddler on how nice the room looks.

Suggestions: At this age it doesn't seem worth a big hassle if she only picks up a few blocks. Consider it a start!

Giving a few minutes' warning before playtime is over helps your toddler adjust to the idea. Remember to be firm, even if she's upset. It'll pay off in the long run.

Picking up right after a play period will help your toddler understand the connection between play and picking up better than if you put it off until later, when she may not even remember playing with the toys.

Cleaning up also worked well as a wind-down activity for Katie since it was usually done before nap or bed.

Variations: Play when other children come to visit, too.

Give older children, friends, or siblings directions more suited to their age. "Pick up all the blue and yellow blocks," "Pick up any round toys," and so forth.

Sing a popular tune with words you make up about picking up toys. "Twinkle, twinkle, here's a block. Now I put it in the box!" (I hope you can come up with something better.)

29

The Bubble Machine

Origin: In an attempt to teach Katie to drink from a cup with a straw, we discovered this very entertaining game.

Equipment: A cup, bucket, or bowl and a straw.

Position: Place the equipment on a table or the floor. Sit with your toddler beside it.

Procedure:

1. Fill the cup with water. Without placing the straw in the water, demonstrate blowing through it. Blow on your toddler's face, her hair, the back of her neck, and her tummy. This is a game in itself!
2. Slowly lower the straw into the water. Say, "Watch me blow bubbles into the water."
3. Blow bubbles in the cup.
4. Hand the straw over to your toddler. First let her just blow air like you did. She can blow on her hand or your hair!
5. Guide the straw into the water.

The Bubble Machine

6. Exclaim excitedly as you see bubbles appear.

7. Once she masters the blowing technique (it may take a few tries), she'll be bubbling up a storm.

Suggestions: Amy and Katie played "The Bubble Machine" in the bath before they soaped up, because Amy was old enough to know not to drink the water and Katie still hadn't figured out how to suck liquid *up* a straw! All this is fine and dandy until your toddler plays "The Bubble Machine" with her milk in the restaurant, right? You need to explain that she can only blow bubbles in water at home. If this doesn't work, remove the straw.

Variations: Show your toddler how to blow bits of paper or cotton balls around with a straw. Get another straw and blow the cotton ball back and forth.

For an older child, there's the trick of filling the straw, holding a finger over one end, and then releasing the water by drops onto paper, sand, or cement to make interesting designs.

30
Copy Cat

Origin: Not satisfied with the small, simple motions of "Monkey See, Monkey Do," we devised these larger actions for our growing toddler.

Equipment: None.

Position: See below.

Procedure:
1. Catch her attention with "Hey! Can you lie on your back and put your legs up?"
2. Hold your position until she's copied you.
3. Now cycle your legs around as if riding a bike. "Can you ride a bicycle?"
4. Wait again for her to catch up.
5. If she's having trouble figuring out how you got into your position, give her some help.
6. Now get tricky. Stand up and say, "Can you jump and clap at the same time?"

7. She'll probably alternate her jumps and claps, but that's okay. Like the old "rub your stomach and pat your head" routine, it's hard to synchronize.

8. From here you can make up any number of "Copy Cat" positions. We enjoyed touching toes, clapping behind our backs, looking between our legs, and many more.

Copy Cat

Suggestions: Jump right into "Copy Cat" if your toddler needs distracting from a bumped
head or hurt feelings. Be sure to let her
catch up with you at every new step.
There's no need to hurry. If she wants to
hold a position (the sillier the better),
that's part of the fun.

Variations: Reverse things by saying, "Now I'll copy
you!"

31
Show and Tell

Origin:	When Katie hit the "What's that?" stage, we decided to find what things she already knew the names of and teach her the names of the others!
Equipment:	None.
Position:	It's easier if you're holding her, but standing alongside is fine, too.
Procedure:	1. We began by asking Katie, "Show me the door." Ask your toddler to point out whatever familiar object you name.
	2. When she points or motions toward the item in question, you say, "Yes! There it is! There's the door."
	3. Walk over to the door.
	4. From this vantage point, look around and find another familiar object for her to identify. "Show me the TV," and "show me the chair" are good ones.

Show and Tell

5. After she recognizes each object, walk over to it, touch it, and say its name again.

6. Now pick some harder items you're not sure she knows. Ask, "Do you know where the vase is?" or "Do you know where the lampshade is?"

7. She may take a wild guess or just say "No." In either case you point it out and say, "There's the vase!" and again walk over to it. But you'll be surprised she knows as much as she does.

Suggestions: Make this a quiet, lazy game by speaking softly as you carry her from spot to spot. Don't forget to steal a few kisses off her soft cheek!

We stuck to "show me" because Katie seemed confused by the term "point to."

Variations: Give your toddler short commands to test and broaden her verbal understanding. "Go get the ball," "Go shut the door," and "Bring me the book" are examples that help you discover how well your toddler understands you.

Play "Show and Tell" outside.

Omit walking to the object and play "Show and Tell" at a restaurant to pass the time between crackers and ice cubes!

32
Fill and Go

Origin: It must have sprung from witnessing the routine fill-up at the gas station, but wherever she got the idea, Katie invented the game "Fill and Go" based on the basic principle that you needed to fill it up to make it go.

Equipment: An assortment of cars or trucks to begin with. After step 6, any variety of objects will work.

Position: Any.

Procedure:
1. Indicating one of your toddler's toy trucks or cars, say, "Do you know what you have to do to make your car go?" Making sure you have her attention, add, "You have to fill it up!"
2. Reach out and pretend to fill up the toy car. Be sure to use the all-important "whoosh" sound effect.
3. After filling the car, scoot it across

Fill and Go

the floor and announce, "There!
Now your car can go!"

4. Now say, "Okay, who's next? I
   must fill up the car if I want it to
   go!" and then fill it up and make it
   go.

5. Continue filling cars and making
   them go. Your toddler may want to
   bring you the cars for you to fill or
   she may want to do the filling herself.

6. Now ask, "What else can I fill up
   and make go?"

7. Look around for something to fill.
   Try filling a chair: "Glug, glug, glug
   . . . I'm filling the chair so it will
   go!"

8. Your toddler may look a little baffled, but when you add, "Now the chair can go!" and scoot it across the floor, she'll get the idea.

9. Fill up a book and make it go by pushing it along the carpeting. Pretend to fill up an apple or orange, and roll it across the floor.

10. Keep repeating, "Fill it up and make it go!"

11. Ask your toddler to bring you something to fill.

12. Fill whatever she brings and say, "Okay, now make it go!"

Suggestions: Although your toddler may enjoy doing some of the filling herself, she'll still want you to be involved in her game. She'll listen for that "whoosh" or "glug, glug" with happy anticipation and then be off!

Variations: In the out-of-doors version of "Fill and Go," fill rocks, sticks, balls, and strollers and watch them go!

Katie loved it when I filled *her* and made *her* go! Fill your toddler with a poke at the tummy or a tug at the back of the pants. I guarantee a laugh.

33
Here's a Hat

Origin: Whereas Amy needed her "blanky" in order to get to sleep, Katie's Achilles' heel was a Hearst's Castle souvenir sailor's cap that she pulled snuggly over her head before drifting off. Whether or not it had anything to do with the fact that she had no hair is hard to say, but hats soon became a favorite pastime.

Equipment: A variety of hats and a mirror.

Position: Pile the hats up on the floor and have a mirror handy.

Procedure:
1. Begin by putting on one of the hats yourself. Say, "How do I look with this hat on?"
2. Look at yourself in the mirror and remark, "Oh! I *like* this hat!" or "Oh, this hat looks silly!"
3. Choose another hat and repeat step 2.
4. Encourage your toddler to try on a hat.

5. This could go either way. Some toddlers don't want to have anything to do with hats. If this is the case, let her try the hats on you! Say, "What hat should I try on now? Can you help me put on a hat?"

6. Look in the mirror together and discuss how the hat looks.

7. If your toddler wants to wear the hats herself, let her choose a hat, and, again, look into the mirror together.

8. Continue trying on hats until you run out of hats or interest.

Here's a Hat

Suggestions: Add a voice change when you're trying on hats, and watch what kind of reaction you get!

Variations: If you have any hats that represent a specific occupation (fire fighter's hat, cowboy hat, etc.), spend a minute talking about that job.

   If an older brother or sister is playing, you're in luck. Amy was such a ham that she kept Katie entertained for ages acting out little stories with each hat.

34
Strolling Along

Origin: Not content to sit in her stroller for more than ten minutes at a time, Katie discovered the following game, which we went along with in order to get from here to there.

Equipment: Stroller, doll, or stuffed animal.

Position: Begin with your toddler, holding her doll or animal, in her stroller (if possible).

Procedure: 1. When your toddler begins to get restless in the stroller, wriggling under the strap or climbing up over the back, suggest, "Why don't you push Teddy (animal or doll) for a while?"

2. Assuming it sounds like a good idea to her, buckle Teddy into the stroller and position your toddler behind it.

3. Pick out a landmark about half a

Strolling Along

block away and say, "Teddy wants
you to push him to that red mailbox."

4. Help her maneuver the stroller
down the sidewalk. She'll probably
want to think she's doing it all by
herself, so be discreet!

5. When you reach the mailbox, say,
"Now Teddy wants to push *you* to
the lamppost" (another half a
block away).

6. You can hope she'll go along with
that idea. If not, let her push Teddy
a little further, and remind her that

after Teddy's turn she'll have another chance to push.

7. Once your toddler is buckled back into the stroller, hold Teddy's paws under your hands so it looks as though he's pushing too.

8. Stroll along to the lamppost, commenting, "Teddy likes to push the stroller. Don't you think he's doing a good job?"

9. Change places at the lamppost, and pick another landmark to aim for.

10. You should be able to make some progress this way, and if you're lucky your toddler will tire of pushing Teddy and be content to ride for a while!

Suggestions: If your toddler is content in her stroller, save "Strolling Along" for a time when you really need it. The idea here is to let sleeping dogs lie.

If you're using the kind of stroller that has a bar on the back, let your toddler stand on this while you position yourself behind her and push. Just the fact that she's standing instead of sitting may be enough.

And if your toddler enjoys pushing the stroller but finds it awkward and frustrating, you may want to invest in a doll buggy or stroller for her to push along and leave her stroller at home.

Variations: If you'd rather keep your toddler in her stroller but need to distract her from thoughts of escape, try changing the pace a little. For example, go fast between driveways but slow down around curves. Or give her a bumpy ride wherever there's a parked car and come to a dead stop at mailboxes. You can plan it out ahead of time or surprise her along the way.

Pretending to crash into trees, retaining walls, or bushes with a last-minute swerve for a harrowing escape will keep her entertained.

An older brother or sister will think of 101 ways to push a stroller, including backwards! So long as they've been briefed on the basic rules of safety and you're within reach, let them take over "Strolling Along."

35
Water Art

Origin: Having been given a clean paint brush to play with by her father, who was painting the trim on the house, Katie did her own painting with gutter water.

Equipment: A variety of paint brushes and a bucket of water.

Position: Place the equipment and your toddler outside on dry cement.

Procedure:
1. Demonstrate the brush stroke by first dipping a brush into the bucket and then running the wet brush along the cement. Say, "Look, Mommy's painting the cement!"
2. Hand your toddler a brush and let her try it.
3. Compliment her efforts: "Good girl! You're painting too!"
4. Paint a circle with water on the cement, saying, "Look, I painted a circle." Then suggest, "Let's paint inside the circle."

5. Help your toddler fill in the circle.

6. Depending on the toddler, you can either continue making shapes or designs to fill in or she may have ideas of her own.

7. Encourage her to try the different brushes. Draw her attention to the different patterns they make.

8. Katie discovered something new each time she played "Water Art," from painting around her foot to dumping out or standing in the bucket!

Water Art

Suggestions: Play this game in warm weather and go barefoot.

    If you've only got a small area to work with, use a cup of water and an old toothbrush.

Variations: This is a good game in which to introduce shapes. Don't expect your toddler to do it, but you can paint and name circles, squares, and triangles.

    Older children will enjoy painting over a leaf and then removing it to find its shape left on the dry cement. Amy even painted over Katie's carefully spread hand which, much to Katie's delight, left a perfect outline on the cement.

36
Grandma's
Garden Game

Origin: One of the best things about going to Grandma's was working in her garden. And since it involved imitation, repetition, and lots of dirt, it was a favorite.

Equipment: A trowel or shovel, bulbs or flowers to plant, a hose or watering can.

Position: Have all the necessary equipment ready at the garden or work site.

Procedure:
1. Ask, "Will you help me plant some flowers?" and hand her her bucket, trowel, and watering can.
2. Demonstrate how to dig a small hole for a flower plant (or poke a finger in for a seed).
3. Now let her try.
4. Once the plant is in place, let her pack the dirt around it and water it with her hose or can.

Grandma's Garden Game

5. Show her where the next hole should be dug.

6. Continue working as a team (she digs, you plant; she packs, you water), trading off jobs as you go.

Suggestions: The dirt and water (yes, that makes mud) may soon have more appeal than the actual planting, so be prepared and dress accordingly.

Variations: Depending on what gardening really needs to be done, this game can be adapted to any activity. Toddlers love to rake as well as weed, so don't hesitate to give her her own tools and put her to work!

A small watering can is a wonderful toy for a toddler. Katie became so attached to ours that pretending to water plants soon became a game in itself. We'd send her off with the instructions, "Go water all the plants," and she'd scamper away happy as a lark.

37
Best Word Book Ever

Origin: We always took several books with us in the car, for even the shortest trips could seem interminable with a toddler. The following procedure is based on the toddler's love of repetition, her fascination with emotions such as happy, sad, mad, and so on, and her constant question, "What's that?"

Equipment: Stories such as *Gingerbread Man, Chicken Little, The Little Red Hen,* and *The Three Pigs* will satisfy the toddler's delight in repetition, and Richard Scary's word books and Gyo Fujikawa's charming picture books will work wonders for labeling places, people, and things.

Position: Snuggle up close for this one.

Procedure (story book): 1. For stories such as *The Little Red Hen,* begin by studying the cover and discussing what the title of the book means. "Do you know what a

Best Word Book Ever

hen is?" or "Have you ever seen a gingerbread man?"

2. Use enough expression when you read so your toddler will know who is talking to whom, but don't overdo it. Many of these stories have some scary characters which, if too dramatically portrayed, will come back to haunt her later.

3. Take time to look at each picture carefully. Name the characters pictured and discuss what they're doing.

4. As soon as you turn the last page, your toddler will probably plead, "Again!" Go ahead. None of these books takes much more than ten minutes to read.

Procedure (picture word book):	**1.** First, let your toddler flip around until she finds a page that interests her.
	2. Point to something on the page and say, "Look, Huckle Cat is riding a bike."
	3. When she points to something or comments on a particular picture, talk about what is happening.
	4. Now find a page that has something spilling, someone falling or crying, or cars crashing.
	5. Point to the picture and say, "Uh-oh!" Your toddler will be fascinated by these incidents and soon seek out the page so she, too, can point to it and say, "Uh-oh!"
	6. Find a page that your toddler can readily identify—a playground, a garden, a farm, or a beach scene—and talk about when she was there.
	7. Many books have pages illustrating "What I want to be when I grow up" or different occupations. These are fun to look at, too.
Suggestions:	Your toddler will have her favorites, and, as boring as it may be, humor her with constant reading. If you want her to love books and enjoy reading them all her life, let her feel the specialness of a favorite book. Along these same lines, remember that looking at books is supposed to be fun. If she learns colors or numbers or sizes along the way, great,

but don't always make storytime into a lesson.

Variations: An older child will enjoy the silly antics of Papa Bear in the Berenstain Bear adventures, and, because they are written in rhyme, she'll soon enjoy saying the last word in the sentence.

Part III

Eighteen to Twenty-One Months

Exploring Toddler Games

Suddenly they're real people! One-and-a-half, if you please. This term seemed to suit our growing Katie much better than "eighteen-month-old." *That* was for babies, and, as you know by now, a one-and-a-half-year-old is no baby! So when you no longer calculate her age by months but by years, you may feel a slight tug on your heart, along with pride and optimism for your small child and what lies ahead for her.

What's ahead is a period of exploration and curiosity. Katie became fascinated with other toddlers, and, although she did not consider herself a baby, this is often how she'd identify her own peers. One way to give your toddler an opportunity to observe other children play as well as getting some firsthand experience in sharing is to form a play group. Getting together once a week with a few friends is not only beneficial for your toddler but can be a lifesaver for Mom, too. It's often a relief to know you're not the only one who loses her patience or your toddler's not the only one who bites! And talking honestly with friends who share your concerns can be a real help in these turbulent and sometimes isolated first few years.

If a play group isn't workable for one reason or another, scout your community for some "Mommy and

Me" programs. Many school districts offer such classes through their recreation departments, and some even include discussion groups and guest speakers as well as music, movement, and outside play for the toddlers. Many gymnastics schools and libraries have special "Mommy and Me" arrangements that are fun for socializing and learning.

If other kids were Katie's first love, then animals were a close second. We took walks looking for a friendly cat stretched out on the sunny sidewalk so Katie could pet its soft fur and scratch its ears. On nice days we fed the ducks bread scraps at a neighborhood pond, and on rainy days we visited the local pet shop. And don't forget the petting zoo! If she's into animals, she'll love it . . . but wait and take Daddy and the camera! Add a picnic lunch to any of the above and you've made a nice morning outing. Now your toddler's ready for a nap, right? Well, let's put it this way: Mom is!

After her nap or bath or dinner, you might find time to play a few games with your exploring toddler.

38

Crab Walks

Origin: Kids love a relaxed target, and Katie is no exception. So, as I leaned back on the floor watching TV, Katie couldn't resist sitting on my stomach. As I rose up into the crab position, Katie laughed and we played as follows.

Equipment: None.

Position: As you sit with knees up and hands back for support, your toddler straddles your stomach as if riding a horse.

Procedure:
1. Begin with "Hey! Did you want to ride a crab?" and raise yourself and your toddler a few inches off the floor.
2. As she feels the motion and loses touch with the floor, she'll probably grab your shoulders and laugh at the unexpected action.
3. "Hang on! This crab is taking you for a ride!" Raise her up and down, or gently swing from side to side.

4. Now take a step forward or backward. If she enjoys the action, keep moving!

5. Then change directions. "Now this crab is going *this* way. You're having quite a crab ride!"

6. Even though giggling Katie could have gone on forever, the crab got tired out! When this happens, lower crab and rider to the ground, saying, "This crab needs to rest before the next riders come!"

Suggestions: "Crab Walks" is an easier riding game than the horse version with the toddler

Crab Walks

on your back. Katie could either hang on to the knees or shoulders of the crab she was riding.

How fast your crab goes should depend on how enthusiastic your toddler is. Fast is fun, but be careful not to topple her off.

Variations: An older sibling will want to ride the crab or even give a ride, depending on his or her age.

Suggest that your toddler give Teddy Bear a ride.

39
Baby Bumble Bee

Origin: This is a song I learned at Girl Scout camp, and it came in quite handy during a longer-than-estimated drive.

Equipment: None.

Position: Any.

Procedure:
1. Facing your toddler, clasp your hands together and begin, "I'm bringing home a baby bumble bee."
2. Sway your hands back and forth, cupped as if you were in fact holding a bumble bee. Continue, "Won't my Daddy be so proud of me. 'Cause I'm bringing home a baby bumble bee."
3. Now comes the fun finish, "Buzzy, buzzy, buzzy, buzzy" (and each "buzzy" is louder than the one before it), "Ow! He stung me!" Give a look of painful surprise as you open your hands on "Ow!"

144

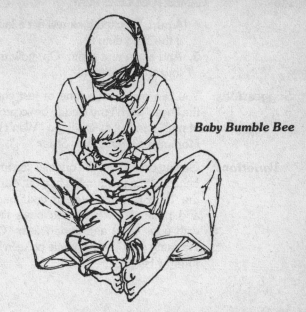

Baby Bumble Bee

4. And again: "I'm bringing home a baby bumble bee.
Won't my Daddy be so proud of me?"
(Cupped hands swaying back and forth.)
"'Cause I'm bringing home a baby bumble bee.
Buzzy, *buzzy*, BUZZY, BUZZY . . .
Ow!"
(Hands fly open in surprise.) "He stung me!"

(A hurt, shocked look will get a laugh
if the sting didn't.)

5. And again and again. Oh, how they
love that repetition!

Suggestions: You can make up a tune or just chant
the lines. "Won't my *Daddy* be so proud
of me!" can just as easily go "Won't my
Mommy or *Grandpa* or *Sister* . . ."

Variations: Getting bored with the original version, I
began letting the bumble bee out during
the "buzzy buzzies" (open your hands
and pretend to follow the bee's flight
with your eyes) and ended with "Ow!
He stung *you!*" and a gentle poke in her
tummy. Hug!

40
Mr. Pig's Wild Ride

Origin: Katie reminded us of this classic that's been around forever when she jumped on Daddy's back as he tied his shoes.

Equipment: None.

Position: The toddler stands on a bed, couch, or chair while the adult stands with his or her back to the toddler.

Procedure: 1. Bending your knees to adjust for height, say, "Okay, hang on while Mr. Pig takes you on his wild ride!" Place your toddler's arms around your neck.
2. Once your toddler has a grip around your neck, reach around and support her bottom with your hands and arms.
3. Now say, "Here we go on Mr. Pig's wild ride!" and slowly walk through the house, adjusting your speed to your particular rider.

Mr. Pig's Wild Ride

4. Here's the silly part. Walk directly toward a wall and say, "Oh no! A wall! It's coming. Will this pig turn or crash into the wall?"

5. Just before reaching the wall, make a quick (but not too quick) turn. "Whew! We turned just in time!"

6. Walking now in a new direction, head for another near miss. "Here

comes a chair! I hope we don't crash into it . . . ohhh!"

7. Once again swerving in the nick of time, say, "Whew! What a wild ride!"

8. If she's enjoying this wild ride, give her a few more laughs, then find a soft spot (couch or bed) to gently dump your rider. "Mr. Pig's wild ride is over at last. Home again, safe and sound."

Suggestions: If your toddler isn't holding on tightly, lean forward as you walk to keep her weight against you.

Variations: The quick turns may be too much for a young toddler. If this is the case, a simple tour through the house, naming rooms and waving to those you pass, is a fun way to introduce piggyback rides.

"Mr. Pig's Wild Ride" can be played outside, almost colliding with trees, fences, or lampposts.

And a simple piggyback ride is fun for a toddler tired of walking.

41
Dress Code

Origin: It started with the shoes. Any pair left lying around our house ended up on Katie, who shuffled around the house feeling quite grown-up. Then she began slipping into Amy's shirts and shorts, three sizes too big! And on the days I folded the family laundry . . . well, Katie figured out ways to wear things that no designer could ever imagine. But when she became frustrated trying to pull on a sock or tuck in a shirt, we'd give a quick lesson in "Dress Code."

Equipment: A pair of tennis shoes or slippers, yours or an older siblings', that slip onto your toddler's feet without untying or buckling. Avoid high heels—small ankles twist too easily and hurt too much. A pair of slip-on pants or shorts a size or so too large. A pull-over shirt or sweatshirt, also a bit oversized.

Position: Lay clothes out in front of your toddler, who is dressed only in her underwear.

Procedure:
1. Begin with the pants. Lay them out on the floor. "Here are pants Katie can put on all by herself!"
2. Have your toddler sit facing the waist opening, and guide one leg into the correct leg opening. "This leg goes in this side."
3. Back off for a minute and see if she can continue on her own. It's a good idea to find out what your child does and doesn't know before teaching her something!

Dress Code

4. Help her slip her other leg into the pants. "In goes this leg. Goodbye, leg!" Still sitting, gather up the pant legs until her feet stick out. "Hey! Where did Katie's feet go? Pull up your pants . . . peek-a-boo! Here they are!"

5. Now she needs to stand. To pull up her pants the rest of the way, help her put one hand in front and one hand in back, and pull. "Pull! Up come your pants." Here, the baggier the better!

6. "Ta da!" Give a big hug and a proud pat on the back. "You are really a big girl. You put your pants on all by yourself!"

7. The shirt is tricky, but if it's loose she can pull it over her head easily. Lay it out like you did the pants.

8. Again, see how she approaches it. "Can you put your shirt on?"

9. Then help her pick up the bottom of the shirt and pull it over her head. "Hey! Where's Katie? Come out of that shirt!" Position the shirt so she can pop her head out of the neck. "There she is!"

10. By now, reaching around for the arm holes is second nature, so let her grope around for a minute to get her arms out. "Pop! Here come the arms!" If the shirt's a bit on the big side, it'll be that much easier.

11. More hugs, pats, and praise.
12. Now for some fun, since she's probably figured out by now that this isn't much of a game! Have ready a pair of adult or older sibling shoes. "Oh yes! Are you going to put on these big grown-up shoes?"
13. Give her a chance to put the shoes on by herself, helping her if she hits a snag.
14. Finish up. "Look! You're all dressed! You dressed yourself!"

Suggestions: This is obviously a game for a rainy, stay-at-home kind of day. Plan ahead before playing to make sure you don't need to hurry or aren't going somewhere immediately following the game. Katie liked to clomp around in her crazy get-up for a while before relinquishing it for a more suitable outfit.

If you have an older child, you'll have larger sizes handy; if not, just be sure the clothes for "Dress Code" are loose enough to slip on easily.

Be sure to intercede or even quit until a later date if your toddler becomes too frustrated.

Variations: If she doesn't already, your toddler may prefer undressing to dressing. Shoes and socks are often the first to go, quickly followed by the pants. It's normal; she *is* learning, and you can play

"Dress Code" after there's nothing left to take off!

Since the shoes seem to be the highlight, any kind of specialty shoes (ballet, tap, soccer) you have around the house will really delight your toddler.

42

Blanket Bubbles

Origin: This time four-year-old Amy started it. As Katie sat on the picnic blanket, Amy began flapping one side up and down. Katie laughed, I grabbed a side, and . . .

Equipment: Large blanket, quilt, or sheet.

Position: The toddler sits in the center of the spread-out blanket. Other players kneel around the edges. "Blanket Bubbles" works well with anywhere from three to five players, but two can get by, and more than five just means more bubbles!

Procedure: 1. Lift the edges of the blanket up and down, letting air ripple under the blanket.
2. Say, "Look at the bubbles!" and encourage your toddler to crawl across the bubbles. "Katie, can you crawl on the bubbles?"
3. She may crawl or she may just sit

there. Adjust the bubbles to her mood and try "Can you *pop* the bubbles?" Demonstrate by slapping your hand on a bubble near you.

4. Encourage her to continue popping bubbles all over the blanket. "Go pop Amy's bubbles! Now get Daddy's bubbles!"

5. Is anything happening? Katie sometimes enjoyed just sitting amidst the bubbles. But you can suggest rolling on the bubbles, jumping, kicking, walking backwards, and so on.

6. Now it's someone else's turn, and your toddler can help make the bubbles.

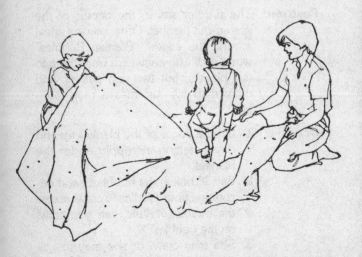

Blanket Bubbles

Suggestions: Don't make your bubbles too big or too fast until your toddler is comfortable playing "Blanket Bubbles."

A grassy area outside is ideal for the game, but it's fun as a rainy-day recess too!

Variations: To begin with, your toddler can go under the blanket while the other players flutter it up and down over her. Or you can pull her along as she sits in the middle hanging on. And, if you've got other adults with you, you can lift her right up off the ground and sway back and forth for a real thrill ride. Then there's throwing a portion of the blanket over her and whipping it off in a quick round of peek-a-boo. So, if "Blanket Bubbles" doesn't turn out to be a huge success, one of the above variations is sure to catch her fancy!

43
Follow the Leader

Origin: Thinking back, this was Amy's idea too. We were taking a walk and, you know kids, Amy just popped out with "I'll be the leader and you have to do what I do!" Needless to say, having one-and-a-half-year-old Katie toddling along set a simple tone for the game.

Equipment: None.

Position: Stand in a line, first adult, then toddler. Or have an older sibling lead and put your toddler in the middle.

Procedure:
1. The leader says, "Okay, everybody! Do what I do." Then slowly walk forward.
2. Toddler follows.
3. Leader jumps three times and says, "Jump! Three jumps!"
4. Leader turns a full circle, saying, "Now turn around."
5. Leader takes followers on a detour

Follow the Leader

around a tree, lamppost, or (if indoors) chair.

6. Leader gets tricky and walks backwards!

7. As long as the toddler is a happy follower, the leader can try clapping hands; walking with hands on her head, hips, or ears; running; touching toes; and so forth.

Suggestions: Be sure to wait for the toddler to complete the trick before going on.

You can use "Follow the Leader" to teach words such as "jump," "clap," "backwards," "behind," "up," or "down."

Variations: Your "Follow the Leader" line-up can be made into a train by either holding on to each other's waists or holding hands. The first person is the big black engine, and the last person, of course, is the little red caboose. Toot, toot!

An older toddler may enjoy being the leader with the help of a "backseat leader."

44

Push 'Em Back

Origin: Katie ran up, hugged my legs, and knocked me off balance, and I flopped onto the couch. My cry of "Hey! You pushed me over!" got such a laugh we tried it again and again.

Equipment: None.

Position: Stand in front of a couch facing your toddler, and have your toddler stand facing you.

Procedure:
1. You start by saying, "Can you push me over? Use your strong arms to push me over!"
2. Brace yourself; they're stronger than they look! Let her push on your legs to the count of three, "One, two, three."
3. Then flop back onto the couch. "Oh! You pushed me over!"
4. Challenge her again, and repeat steps 2 and 3.

5. This time get tricky. "Well, can you push me over with your *back?*"

6. Encourage her to figure out how to back up to your legs. "Turn around and push with your *back!*"

7. And when her back does press against you, fall onto the couch, saying, "Hey! You pushed me over with your back!"

8. Here's Katie's favorite: "Push with your *eyes* closed!" or "Push with your *ear!*" And "Push with one hand" will take some thinking.

9. Call it quits when you're "pushed out"!

Push 'Em Back

Suggestions: As you fall back, your toddler may fall on top of you. Allow for a smooth landing.

Variations: Big brothers or sisters can get into the act by letting a toddler push them.

If you've got extra adults and toddlers, line up the adults and let the toddlers push them all back at the same time.

45
Horsie

Origin: Amy, four-and-a-half, was determined to be in charge of a game. So she picked her favorite, playing the horse instead of the rider and adding a few new twists.

Equipment: None.

Position: Amy lay flat on the floor, face down. Katie knelt beside her.

Procedure:
1. "Okay, Katie! Hop on me!" called Amy. And Katie straddled this flattened pony.
2. Then Amy announced, "If you want me to get up, you have to turn the crank." This was the first we'd heard of a crank-up horse (where do kids get these ideas?), but we helped Katie turn an imaginary crank near her horse's side.
3. And what do you know? As we cranked, the horsie slowly rose up on all fours! You should have seen

Horsie

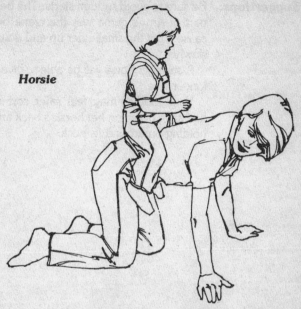

Katie's face as she hung on for dear life.

4. "Now say, 'Giddy-up, go,' Katie" directed Amy. Katie did, and Amy took a few staggering steps forward.
5. "You say 'Whoa!' to make me stop," said Amy, who didn't realize her rider would be so heavy. "And then turn the crank again," Amy added.
6. Katie, horsewoman that she is, said, "Whoa!" and we helped her turn the crank.
7. Amy sank slowly to the floor. The ride was over.

Suggestions: Be sure to avoid sudden starts. The best part of Amy's game was the crank because it got the small rider up and down slowly.

A stronger horse will be able to give a longer ride.

Your toddler may feel safer sort of half lying down on her horsie's back and holding on around its neck.

46
The Name Game

Origin: How many times has someone sidled up to your cart while grocery shopping and asked your toddler, "Well, hello. What's your name?" Katie must have been asked that five times a day, in line at the drug store, over at the post office, and even at the drive-up bank teller! And even though she knew perfectly well what her name was and had just been talking a blue streak, she'd immediately clam up and hide her face in her hands. So we made up a game to break the ice.

Equipment: None.

Position: Any.

Procedure:
1. Catch your toddler off guard as she enters a room, or say to her at the dinner table, "Hello, little girl! What's your name?"
2. Your toddler will probably giggle and may or may not answer, but encour-

The Name Game

age her to say her name. "Can you tell me your name? Say, 'Katie.' "

3. After she says her name, you respond, "Oh, Katie. That's a pretty name! How old are you Katie?"

4. More giggles? Say, "You're one. Can you say 'one'?"

5. Then show her how to hold one finger up to indicate that she is one. "You're one year old! See?"

6. Now remind her of her recent experience, "Remember that lady in the

market who said, 'What's your
name?' " Pause. "But you forgot to
say 'Katie'!"

7. Now repeat the "What's your
name?" and "How old are you?"
questions.

8. Give her a round of applause and a
hug!

Suggestions: Don't push her if she just doesn't want
to "perform," but she may feel more
comfortable in those awkward situations
if she knows her lines!

She can fall back on her "Name
Game" experience when meeting new
friends, young or old, and it's good
training for when she eventually must
learn formal introductions.

Variations: You can play "The Name Game" while
she's in her car seat or at a restaurant.
And you can always add to it "Where's
Mommy? Where's Daddy?"

An older toddler may enjoy learning
and reciting other family names. Does
she know Grandma's first name? They
always get a kick out of that!

47

Inside, Outside, Around

Origin: Amy had a hula hoop, and when Katie got her turn she just wanted to stand inside it, outside it, or on top of it.

Equipment: A hula hoop is nice to have, but a circle of masking tape about three feet across works just as well.

Position: Tape your circle onto the carpet, sidewalk, or patio, and stand inside it. Your toddler is watching.

Procedure:
1. "Look, Katie! Mommy is *inside* the circle! Can you step inside the circle with me?"
2. She does, and you say, "Hey, we are both inside the circle."
3. Suggest, "Let's step *outside* our circle." Take her hand and step outside the circle together.
4. Step *on top of* the circle, and have your toddler follow your lead. "We are on top of the circle."

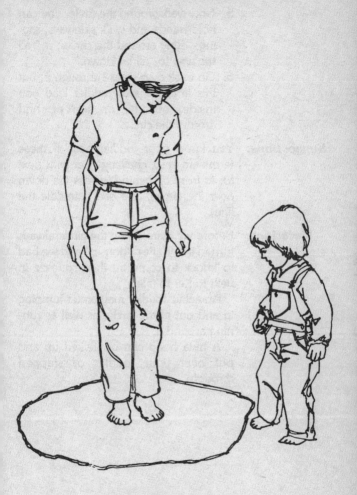

Inside, Outside, Around

5. Now walk *around* the circle. You can hold hands and walk sideways, saying, "Ring around the circle . . ." all the way to "all fall down."

6. Go back over steps 1 through 5, but this time let your toddler lead you inside, outside, on top of, and around the circle.

Suggestions: You know your toddler best. If these terms are easy, challenge her with *next to, in front of, behind, across* (lie down over the circle), and *over* (straddle the line).

Variations: Before we were done, the circle always turned into Katie's "house;" and we had to knock to come in, then squeeze in next to her to talk.

An active toddler may prefer jumping in and out of the circle, as well as running around it.

A hula hoop can be picked up and put *over* your toddler or stepped *through*.

48
Tot's Bowling

Origin: Like most everything, it was an accident when Katie rolled her big rubber ball into Amy's carefully made block building. But it gave us an idea, and after we helped Amy reconstruct her masterpiece we played "Tot's Bowling."

Equipment: You can use any size ball for the bowling ball, but the bigger the better. The bowling pins can be anything from stacked blocks to empty coffee cans (see below).

Position: Stack or line up blocks, bottles, or cans, and then take about five giant steps backward.

Procedure:
1. Demonstrate rolling the ball along the ground or floor toward the pins. "Here I go! I'm rolling my ball at the blocks!"
2. Hope that you knock something down so you can cheer, "Hurrah! I knocked it over!"

Tot's Bowling

3. Now it's your toddler's turn. "Here, you roll the ball at the blocks."

4. Whether she knocks anything down or not, cheer enthusiastically.

5. Encourage her to roll again, stepping closer if she missed the first time. "Okay, step up and roll again!"

6. Set up the pins for the next round, adjusting height or spacing as needed.

Suggestions: Taking turns with your toddler will not only help her learn that important skill but will also give her a chance to watch and copy you as you roll for a strike.

Variations: If you're outside at the beach or a park, sticks stuck into sand or dirt can act as pins.

Once we introduced sticks to the game, all Katie wanted to do was hit our big ball with her stick, chase it, hit it . . . the original object of the game was lost on her!

We coined Katie's variation "Stick Ball," but kicking the ball at the pins also makes a fun change of pace.

Older children enjoy the challenge of knocking over pins. Make them take a few steps back, though, as they become more proficient.

49
Taps

Origin: It started because, instead of clapping her hands like we usually did when singing "Old McDonald Had a Farm," Katie sat down and clapped on her legs. So Amy tapped on *her* head . . .

Equipment: Music. You can either provide it yourselves by singing a familiar tune or put on a record, children's or adult's, instrumental or vocal.

Position: Sit beside your toddler on the floor.

Procedure:
1. As soon as the music starts, begin to clap your hands.
2. If she hasn't joined you, encourage her to do so. "Clap your hands to the music!"
3. Now switch to tapping on top of your head.
4. Again, have her follow your lead by calling to her, "Tap your head!"
5. After a few head taps, move down to the tummy.

6. "Tap on your tummy!" you say to her.

7. Reach down to your toes next. "Oh! Can you tap on your toes?"

8. Continue finding new locations to tap, keeping in time to the music and naming the part of the body you're tapping. Katie enjoyed tapping her nose, ears, knees, shoulders, chin, and behind her back.

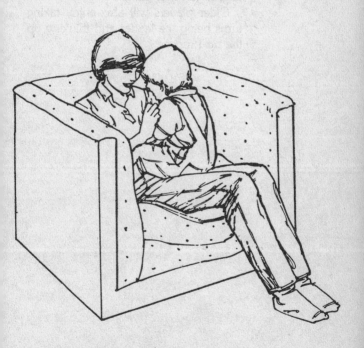

Taps

Suggestions: "Taps" can be played in a car by either turning on the radio or having a sing-along.

"Taps" is a sneaky way to teach your toddler some parts of the body she's unfamiliar with.

Variations: Make "Taps" a challenge for older children by naming and then tapping more obscure spots like the calves, shins, thighs, gums, or palms.

Older players will also enjoy taking turns being the leader and thinking up the next moves.

50
Add-a-Word

Origin: Along about now, Katie began putting words together into two- and even three-word sentences. We played the following game to encourage these verbal skills and to sneak in a lesson in size and color.

Equipment: None.

Position: Any.

Procedure:
1. Begin when your toddler makes one of her one-word demands: "more," "again," or "up."
2. Say, "More? More what? More cat food?" Laugh to let her know you're just teasing. "More mudpies? More peanut butter soup?"
3. You should have induced a giggle. Now encourage her to complete her sentence by adding what it is she really wants more of. "Oh! More juice! Why didn't you say so?"

Add-a-Word

4. Give a big hug.
5. Now add another word to the sentence by asking, "What kind of juice is this? Is it orange juice? Apple juice? Banana juice?"
6. Answer the question for her if she hesitates or seems confused.
7. Now put it all together. Say, "Oh, you want more *apple* juice, right?"
8. Encourage her to say all three words. Give her another big hug and, finally, more apple juice!

Suggestions: Whenever your toddler speaks in one-word sentences, encourage her to finish the thought. Some toddlers get lazy in their speech if you too readily understand their one-word requests. But don't make a big issue out of it, or she'll clam up on you! Just having you say the whole sentence will set an example.

Variations: This is a good way to introduce "please" and "thank you" into your toddler's vocabulary. It will soon become automatic.

When your toddler identifies something in one word, "doggie" for example, show her how to use words to describe the dog. Ask her, "Is it a big dog or a little dog?" and so on. This works for "hot" and "cold," "happy" and "sad," and color comparisons too.

51
Small World

Origin: One of Katie's favorite toys at this age was her Fisher-Price busload of people. Next came the ferris wheel. The variety of people included in the Fisher-Price set (a grandmother, a daddy, a sister, a cross-looking boy) lent itself to the following role-play game.

Equipment: Any kind of play set that includes people, a car, a bus, or some kind of transportation.

Position: Place some of the people in the bus. Line up the others as if they were waiting for a turn to get on.

Procedure: 1. Suggest that your toddler be the bus driver. Add, "I'll help the people get on the bus."
2. One at a time, walk one of the little people into the bus.
3. The grandmother might say, "Oh, I hope the bus driver doesn't go too fast!" The cross-faced boy might

push, and the daddy could say, "Uh-oh! I'm late for work!, We'd better hurry!"

4. Once everyone is loaded into the bus, let your toddler drive it over to wherever you and she had decided would be the drop-off point.

5. When Katie played, this was where the ferris wheel came in. Bus passengers would disembark and then line up for a turn on the ferris wheel. But any kind of activity can take the place of the ferris wheel, even another bus or a bowl that is pretending to be a swimming pool.

6. Unload the bus passengers in the same manner as you loaded them, issuing comments from each.

7. Your toddler can now either drive

Small World

the empty bus around and then return for her passengers or help her little people onto the ferris wheel.

8. Repeat the loading and unloading of the bus until your toddler invents her own variation of "Small World."

Suggestions: Be sure to stress taking turns and waiting in line. Your toddler probably hears that a lot herself and will enjoy seeing it acted out. The same is true of pushing in line. Your toddler will delight in the reprimand of the cross-faced boy by the grandmother!

Variations: Instead of a ferris wheel or some such activity at the end of the line, have each passenger go off to school, work, home, the store, and so on.

A bus crash will liven things up, too!

52
Shampoo-Do

Origin: While Katie enjoyed her bath, she sometimes resisted having her hair washed. "Shampoo-Do" did wonders in distracting her.

Equipment: Shampoo, hand mirror.

Position: Your toddler is in the bath while you sit beside it.

Procedure:
1. Begin by asking, "How about a shampoo-do?" Then explain, "That's a hairdo with shampoo!"
2. Before she can object, lather up her hair until it's nice and foamy.
3. Say, "My! What beautiful white hair you have! Feel your nice, soft hair."
4. Guide her hands up to the lather.
5. Now make little spikes out of the lather on her head.
6. Announce, "There! A lovely shampoo-do!"
7. Use the hand mirror to show her what you've created.

8. Rub away the spikes and design a new do.

9. Be sure to let her see herself!

Suggestions: Rinsing a toddler's hair can be tricky. You can tilt the head back or lean it forward, but we found that letting Katie hold a wash cloth to her eyes helped immensely.

If your toddler is reluctant to have her hair done, demonstrate on a doll or, better yet, an older sibling.

Variations: Foam from a bubble bath can also be molded into interesting shapes, clumped onto heads and shoulders, or tunneled through.

After a while Katie found it was more fun to reach up to her lather-covered head and scoop up a handful of soap to be blown through the air like dandelions.

186

53

In the Driver's Seat

Origin: What toddler isn't fascinated by the driver's seat? Whether it's the buttons, dials, and lights or the steering wheel itself, some young kids could sit for hours pretending to drive.

Equipment: One large saucepan lid, two chairs.

Position: Position the two chairs so they're facing each other. This is your car. The saucepan lid is the steering wheel.

Procedure:
1. Set up the car as described above.
2. Hand your toddler the saucepan lid and ask, "How would you like to take a drive?"
3. Seat your toddler on the chairs as shown in the illustration.
4. Hand her a set of pretend (or real) keys and indicate an imaginary ignition site.
5. Volunteer the starting sound effects, "Vroom!" After this, your

In the Driver's Seat

toddler will probably prefer to make her own.

6. Wave goodbye and call out, "Drive carefully!"

7. After she's driven around a while, ask, "Where are you going?"

8. Depending on her reply ("to the store," "to work," or "to school"), discuss with her what she might see along the way.

9. You can even call out, "Oh! Look out for that dog on the corner! Whew! That was close!"

10. Your toddler will soon have her own ideas of what to do "In the Driver's Seat."

Suggestions: Stress the importance of seatbelts by having her buckle up before starting off.

Variations: Katie hated to travel alone, so she'd scoot up the chairs to make room for her passenger, a teddy bear.

And when Amy was in the driver's seat and Katie was the passenger, it became more like a race than a Sunday drive. Katie loved it.

54

Trap Door

Origin: Once, as Katie was crawling between my legs as children love to do, I closed them around her, trapping her. She thought that was quite funny.

Equipment: None.

Position: Stand in a straddle position. Have your toddler nearby.

Procedure:
1. Call to your toddler, "Hey, why don't you go under my bridge?"
2. She'll do it, trust me.
3. Let her scamper through untouched.
4. Then suggest she try it again.
5. This time, as she's crawling between your legs, tighten them around her waist.
6. Cry out, "Aha! Trapped you!"
7. Release your hold on her right away, and say, "You never know when the trap door will close on you!"

Trap Door

8. Now it becomes a game of suspense. Will you or won't you shut the door?
9. Trap her the next time through, but then let her pass freely two times.
10. Continue to play as long as there's interest and your legs hold out.

Suggestions: Pretend to close your legs but then leave them open, only to trap her at the last minute.

   If you close your legs late and clip just her feet, say, "Oh! She slipped past, but I'll get her next time!"

Variations: This game can become almost anything, as you'll find out. Somehow we came up with a version not unlike the windmill at a miniature golf course. I would open and close my legs at regular intervals, and Katie would have to time her dash through just right.

191

55
Toss!

Origin: Amy's preschool teacher gave her a beanbag for Christmas, but it was Katie who had the most fun with it. Since throwing it into a can or basket was too hard for Katie, we designed the following game.

Equipment: One beanbag.

Position: Stand with your toddler in front of a dresser with one drawer pulled partway out.

Procedure:
1. Stand behind your toddler in front of the drawer. Say, "Let's see if we can get this beanbag into that drawer."
2. With her hand in yours, guide her through an underarm motion, dropping the beanbag into the drawer as you come up.
3. Now let her try it on her own.
4. Whether she makes it or not, cheer loudly.

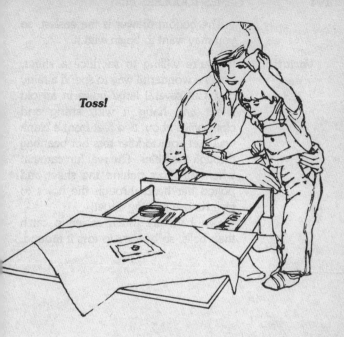

Toss!

5. Stand by the dresser to recover the beanbag. Tossing it back to her can become a game in itself.
6. Close the drawer and try another one, lower or higher, depending on your toddler's preference.
7. You could probably let her play, "Toss!" on her own at this point and go get dinner started!

Suggestions: You could use a small plastic or Nerfball, but a beanbag doesn't roll away or bounce and is easier for a toddler to grip.

The bottom drawer is the easiest, so you may want to begin with it.

Variations: If you're willing to sacrifice a sheet, here's a wonderful way to spend a rainy day. Cut several large holes in an old sheet and hang it with string and clothespins about two feet from a blank wall. Let your toddler toss her beanbag through the holes. The real fun came in when Amy got behind the sheet and poked her head through the holes to give Katie a moving target!

Beanbags are much easier to catch than balls, so be sure to toss it around.

56

One, Two,
Buckle My Shoe

Origin: This is one we learned in a "Mommy and Me" toddler class. It always got a laugh.

Equipment: None.

Position: Stand facing your toddler.

Procedure:
1. Raise both arms above your head and say, "One, two."
2. On "two," stretch your hands down to your toes, keeping your legs straight.
3. Wait for your toddler to catch up with you.
4. Continue, "Buckle my shoe," and pretend to be buckling your shoe.
5. Encourage your toddler to do the same. "Buckle your shoe!"
6. Next comes, "Three, four, shut the door." For this, walk your hands

One, Two, Buckle My Shoe

out in front of you. On "three,"
your right hand moves forward.
On "four," the left hand moves up
so it's even with the right.

7. Keep your legs straight. (See illustration.)
8. To "shut the door," bring your
   hand across in a sweeping motion
   as if you were shutting a door.
9. For "Five, six, pick up sticks," move
   your hands even further out ahead
   of you and pretend to pick up
   some sticks.
10. Again, let your toddler get to this
    point too.
11. The game ends with "Seven, eight,
    lay them straight." Walk your

hands out as far as they'll go while reciting, "Seven, eight."

12. And on "lay them straight," flop dramatically onto your stomach. This is what makes the game worthwhile, so be sure to flop with a lot of oomph.

13. Now you can do it again, a little faster this time.

Suggestions: Don't expect your toddler's legs to stay straight for long!

Variations: Amy continued the nursery rhyme, making up all sorts of movements for "a big fat hen" and "dig and delve." But it was the "lay them straight" flop that remained a favorite part.

Part IV

Twenty-One to Twenty-Four Months

Growing Toddler Games

As your toddler winds up her year of toddlerhood, there will be a surge of eager curiosity and endless energy. It helps if she has outlets for her energy and challenges for her curiosity.

A good place to release some energy is outside, and the best outside toy is a ride toy. They are a toddler's best friend right now and come in all shapes and sizes. There are poodles on wheels, three-wheeled scooters, Big Wheels, wagons, and even motorcycles. Some have pedals, and some you just scoot along with your feet, which works out well since pedals are still pretty tricky for most toddlers. The toddler who gets a lot of fresh air and exercise will probably sleep better, giving you a well-deserved break! And don't forget the park. The slide may be more manageable now than it was a few months ago, and many parks have small swings as well as other toddler-oriented play equipment.

At home you can try introducing Play-doh. Roll it out and let her feel it, squeeze it, and bang on it. Making impressions on a flattened area of Play-doh is something your toddler can do on her own. Blocks, snap beads, and toy cars all make interesting designs when pressed down. But if she can't remember not to eat it, put it away for a few months!

When she's in one of her more curious moods, explore things with her and acknowledge her questions with real answers. No more baby talk for this grown-up toddler! You may feel foolish explaining how Big Bird got inside the TV or where the moon goes during the day, but keep in mind that toddlers love to be talked to and understand more than you think.

Life should be all kinds of fun with your energy-filled toddler and her probing mind . . . except that she can be so stubborn, so assertive, so, so . . . obstinant! Right? And she should be, for she's trying to figure out who she is and how she fits into a world that keeps changing as her perception of it grows. And because she's a little uncertain how to bridge that gap between babyhood and child-hood, she tests her limits over and over again just to see where she stands, or at least to see if *you* know where she stands! Yes, you guessed it, the terrible twos are just around the corner. But they're not so terrible as all that if you stick to your guns during the hard days and give out lots of praise and love on the good ones.

Some activities to consider, if you haven't already, are simple wooden puzzles, listening to records, coloring on big sheets of paper, and, every mother's favorite, "Sesame Street."

And when it's time to play, you'll find the following games bring out the best in your growing toddler.

57
Hide 'n' Seek

Origin: It was Katie's daddy's favorite game as a boy, and he couldn't wait to teach it to her. Here's the version he came up with, suitable for toddlers and really desperate daddies!

Equipment: No equipment is necessary, but, because your toddler may find it difficult to count and hunt on her own, you'll need three players.

Position: See below.

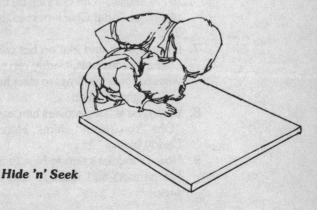

Hide 'n' Seek

Procedure:

1. Explain, "Daddy is going to hide, and we are going to find him! But we have to close our eyes while he goes to hide."

2. Toddler and "partner" bury their faces in the couch or turn to the wall.

3. Say, "We have to count to ten, and then we go find Daddy." Begin, "One, two, three," and encourage her to count along with you.

4. Meanwhile, Daddy has found a very simple hiding spot. Behind a chair, around the corner, or under a table are good ones.

5. Once toddler and partner reach "ten," they set out to seek Daddy. "Okay, let's go find Daddy! Where is Daddy?"

6. Walk slowly through the room, suggesting likely spots for your toddler to investigate. "Oh! Go look by the plant!" or "Aha! Check next to the TV!"

7. If she doesn't find him on her own after a few minutes, Daddy can always cough a few times to steer her in the right direction.

8. When she at last discovers him, say, "Oh! You found him! Here's Daddy hiding!"

9. Now it's toddler's turn to hide (with her partner) and Daddy's turn to seek.

10. As Daddy begins counting, you and the toddler scurry off to find a hiding place. Behind a curtain or a partially opened door is a good spot for two!

11. When Daddy's done counting and as he comes in search of the toddler, he should really ham it up. "Hmmm . . . where's that Katie? I'll bet she's under the table! No? Well, then, she must be behind the couch! No?"

12. The hardest part will be keeping the toddler quiet. Katie always called out, "Here I am!" Try to remind her to hide quietly.

13. After a few false guesses, Daddy finds the toddler, surprise, surprise!

14. Let her have a few more turns hiding and seeking, changing partners if you want.

Suggestions: If you have an older sibling skilled at the game, you don't need two adults.

When hiding places become more elaborate, count to ten two times.

Variations: Katie's daddy always wanted to play so that when you found him he would leap out at you with a shout! His father played it this way with him when he was a boy, but no one in our family has ever wanted to play that way—too scary! Poor Daddy!

58
Freeze

Origin: When Amy wanted to play "Red Light, Green Light" with the family, we had to revise it so Katie could be included. The first variation was called "Stop, Go" (see below), but even this was a bit tricky. So we narrowed it down to "Freeze," which suits toddlers and older children alike.

Equipment: A record or tape.

Position: Players stand in a group, with an adult in charge of the record player.

Procedure:
1. Explain, "When I play the music, you dance. Wave your arms and kick up your legs! But when the music stops, you FREEZE!"
2. Demonstrate by doing a quick jig and then freezing in your dance position.
3. Put on music and encourage your toddler to dance along. Say, "Come on! Stretch your arms up high . . .

Freeze

touch the floor . . . turn around," as you, of course, perform the above routine.

4. Stop the music and freeze in your dance position. Say, "Freeze! You stop when the music stops."
5. Start up the music and dancing again. There's all kinds of dancing fun for a toddler to imitate. Try tippy-toes, twirling, or a heel-and-toe step.
6. Stop the music and call "Freeze!" again.
7. Continue a few more rounds. She'll catch on quickly.

Suggestions: It helps to have older players. They love to freeze in silly-looking positions and can really jazz up the game.

This is a great game for developing your toddler's listening skills. She has to dance and listen for the music to stop, both at the same time. It won't be easy!

Variations: "Stop, Go" is played just like "Red Light, Green Light" except for substituting the words "stop" and "go" for "red light" and "green light." One player is the leader and stands about ten feet in front of the other players. When the leader calls "Go!" the players can walk toward the leader, but when she says "Stop!" they must stop. The game is over when all the players have reached the leader.

This may be too difficult for your toddler right now, but try it after her second birthday and you'll be surprised how much better she does.

"Freeze" is like musical chairs in that your signal for stopping and starting is the music. Katie enjoyed a watered-down version of musical chairs in which there's a chair for each player.

59
Let's Face It!

Origin: When Katie was first learning to draw, faces were her favorite. But they didn't always turn out quite right; noses, eyes, and mouths got all mixed up. "Let's Face It!" helped her put order into the madness.

Equipment: Paper and crayons.

Position: Sit beside your toddler at a low work table.

Procedure:
1. Begin by saying, "Let's draw a picture of Katie!"
2. Draw a large circle on your toddler's paper and say, "There is your head. Can you draw your blue eyes?"
3. Help her find the proper colored crayon, and then, steering her hand to the right general area, let her make a stab at adding the eyes.
4. Compliment her, "Oh, yes! Those are Katie's big blue eyes!"

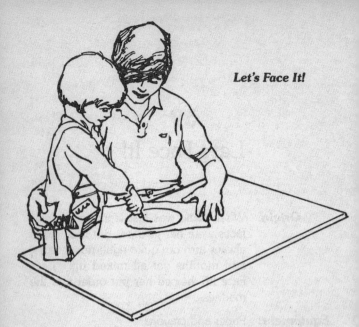

5. Continue, "Now Katie needs a nose. Where should the nose go?"
6. Again, either guide her hand or point to where the nose goes.
7. "Let's use red for Katie's mouth." Help her select the appropriate color, and then indicate where the mouth should be.
8. Ask your toddler what color her hair is and if it's curly or straight.
9. Let her fill in the hair.
10. Hold up the picture, and praise her for a job well done.
11. Suggest, "Do you want to try a picture of Daddy?"

12. Start with a large circle, and then add the eyes, nose, mouth, and hair, as above.

Suggestions: Stick to the basics in the beginning (eyes, nose, mouth, and hair). Then, when your toddler's ready, add ears, eyelashes, cheeks, teeth, and so on.

Take this opportunity to work on color recognition. Talk about the colors of the crayons, hair, eyes, and even the clothes she's wearing.

Variations: After your toddler has finished drawing her face, you can add her body.

For some easy beginning drawing ideas, help your toddler draw the sun, mountains, rain, or flowers.

60
String-O

Origin: When I was growing up, we had a wonderful Airdale dog who used to chase us as we ran down the beach dragging a bamboo stick in the sand. We liked to think he was following the line in the sand, and we called this game "String-O." Watching Katie at the beach pulling her stick behind her reminded me of my "String-O" days. So we played it at the beach that day, and when we got home we made up the following version.

Equipment: Masking tape.

Position: See below.

Procedure:
1. Begin with a straight masking tape line on the carpet, floor, or sidewalk.
2. Say, "Can you follow my line? Walk on the tape!" and demonstrate if necessary.
3. Now curve the line to the right or left.

4. Have your toddler go back to the beginning and follow this new course.
5. Now that she's caught on to the game, you can continue your line. Weave it around the room while your toddler follows right behind you.
6. Talk to her as you lay out the line, "Around we go! Follow my line . . .

String-O

across the floor, around the lamp, up the stairs . . . stay on the line!"

7. You can end up back at the beginning, in your toddler's room, or out the front door.

8. Leave the tape down for a while. She may enjoy following it on her own.

Suggestions: Rather than tearing the tape into segments, leave it on the roll and use one continuous strip. It's easier to pull up this way.

Variations: Don't forget our original "String-O," a stick drawn through the sand at the beach. Dirt at a park or campground works well, too. It also motivates a dawdling toddler to move along!

If you're interested in further developing your toddler's sense of balance, set up a low balance beam (a four-by-four piece of lumber covered with indoor/outdoor carpeting works great) for her to walk across. As any reading specialist will tell you this is a first step in prereading skills.

Low retaining walls and curbs are irresistible to children. When you can afford the time, let them balance across these, holding your hand. It's as good for them as it is fun.

61
Balloon Blasts

Origin: When Katie saw a partially blown-up balloon fly out of my mouth and spin crazily around the room, her laughter was contagious. I'd forgotten how funny that looked.

Equipment: Balloons.

Position: Any.

Procedure:
1. Hold out a balloon and say, "Do you want to see a balloon blast?"
2. Puff three or four breaths into the balloon.
3. Hold the balloon up above your head, say, "Here goes!" and let it go.
4. Follow its erratic flight with a pointed finger, calling, "There it goes! Look at it fly!"
5. Either retrieve the balloon yourself or see if your toddler can find it.
6. Ask, "How about another balloon blast? Shall we make it fly again?"

Balloon Blasts

7. Blow the balloon up a little fuller this time for a longer flight.
8. Let her rip with a cry of "Blast off!"
9. "Balloon Blasts" should hold her attention for several blasts.

Suggestions: If you can get the balloon transferred from your hand to hers, let your toddler release it for blastoff.

Variations: Older children find "Balloon Blasts" entertaining, and if they can blow up the balloon themselves they can take over for a few blasts!

62
Footsie

Origin: Grandma caught on quickly to game playing, and when Katie initiated her foot action Grandma had a few surprises of her own!

Equipment: None.

Position: Either sit on the floor, feet to feet, or face each other as you sit in chairs.

Procedure:
1. Give your toddler's foot a little jab with yours.
2. Look surprised and say, "Oops! Did I get you?"
3. Another jab. Another look of innocent surprise.
4. If she doesn't take the initiative to jab you back, say, "Are you going to play 'Footsie' with me? Try to kick my foot!"
5. When she does try to kick your foot, quickly dodge her blow. "Oh! You missed me!"
6. This ought to get a laugh.

7. Give her one of your quick jabs, and say, "Oops! I got you again!"

8. She may try to kick you again, in which case be sure to dodge her attempt, or she may want you to repeat your jabs.

9. As you continue to play "Footsie," sometimes dodge her kick and sometimes let her get you; sometimes jab her back and sometimes just pretend to. It's the surprise of the unexpected that will make "Footsie" fun!

Suggestions: It's just a game, so don't get too rough!

Variations: You can play the same game using hands instead of feet. When her hands are resting on the table or floor, put one of yours on top of hers. Pull it away, look surprised, and repeat.

63
Spring Cleaning

Origin: Naturally, whatever I was doing looked like more fun than what Katie was doing. So when I swept or dusted, Katie wanted to have a piece of that action.

Equipment: Your own broom and dustpan and a scaled-down version for your toddler, if possible.

Position: Set up your toddler with her equipment wherever you plan to clean.

Procedure:
1. Demonstrate your sweeping technique, and say, "Are you going to help me sweep the floor?"
2. Adjust her hands on her broom so she has a good grip, and guide her in a few strokes. "Push the broom along the floor. Help Mommy sweep!"
3. Sweep all around her before she scatters the crumbs under the kitchen table even further!

Spring Cleaning

4. Demonstrate the dustpan end of sweeping, and then, because she is too small to manipulate both broom and dustpan, hold the dustpan while she sweeps into it, or vice versa.
5. Let her empty the dustpan into the trash.
6. Sweep up where she spilled the dustpan!
7. Let her continue to follow you on your sweeping rounds.

Suggestions: Your chores may take a little longer with this toddling help, but at least you won't have the frustration of having to stop every few minutes to see what your toddler's gotten into, and she will be happier being included in what you're doing.

Variations: Dusting is a good "Spring Cleaning" job for your toddler. Hand her a rag similar to yours, pour a shot of polish on it, and assign her a nice low coffee table to rub.

What Katie really wanted to help with was the windows or mirrors. It was the squirt bottle she was impressed with, so I filled an empty squirter with plain water and let her squirt and then wipe her closet doors, her work table, and the formica kitchen table. You may have to go over these areas to eliminate streaks and puddles, but it was worth it as it kept Katie busy for a long time.

You can even send her outside with her squirt bottle to clean the swingset or patio furniture!

64

Do You Want to See My Sad Face?

Origin: Once, as Katie puckered up her face to cry, I said, "Oh! What a sad face! Do you want to see *my* sad face?" And that made her forget to cry and started us off on a new game.

Equipment: Mirror.

Position: Sit in front of the mirror.

Procedure:
1. Look into the mirror and say, "Do you want to see my sad face?"
2. Make a terribly sad face into the mirror.
3. Say, "Oh! How sad that was! Can *you* make a sad face? Look in the mirror and show me your sad face."
4. She does, and you exclaim, "Oh, that *is* sad!" and laugh.
5. Continue, "Now do you want to see my happy face?" Big smile.

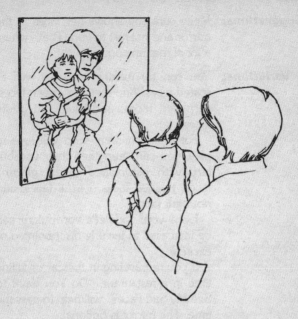

Do You Want to See My Sad Face?

6. And then, "Show me *your* happy face!"
7. Laugh, "Oh, I like that happy face!"
8. Now show her your mad face. "Here is my *mad* face. Grrr!"
9. Ask, "Can *you* make a mad face?"
10. After she demonstrates her mad face, say, "Oh! That *is* mad. Look in the mirror at that mad face!"
11. Laugh, hug, and say, "We made all different faces!"

Suggestions: Make sure she shows her faces in the mirror and not just to you. That's where a lot of the fun comes in!

Variations: You can try making scary as well as scared faces. And there are mean faces, surprised faces, and plain old goofy faces.

For older children, who will love to play, you can strengthen their vocabulary with *astonished* faces, *gloomy* faces, *puzzled* faces, *wistful* faces, and *doubtful* faces.

Even your toddler's vocabulary can be increased to include *disappointed* or *excited.*

If you're traveling in the car or killing time in a restaurant, "Do You Want to See My Sad Face?" will help to pass the time. The mirror is optional.

65

Obstacle Course

Origin: It started out simply enough as I requested that the children walk around the stacks of folded laundry, not into them! Then Amy made a game of it, with Katie catching on quickly.

Equipment: Several dish towels, wash clothes, or scarves, a low stool or stepstool, and a chair.

Position: Line up the towels a few feet apart. Next comes the chair, then the stool, and you're set.

Procedure:
1. Standing by the towels, say, "Okay, here I go on an obstacle course!"
2. Go around the towels, go under the chair (tight fit?), step up on the stool, jump off, run and touch the wall, and go back to where you started.
3. "There! Did you see me? I went around the towels, up on the stool, and touched the wall." Ask, "Do you want to go on the obstacle course?"

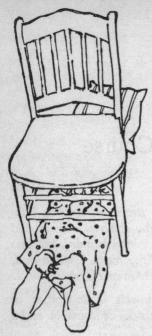

4. Take your toddler's hand and walk her through it, explaining, "Walk *around* the towels . . . *under* the chair . . . *up* on the stool . . . jump! . . . touch the wall . . . and back to the beginning!"
5. Now let her try it on her own.
6. Let her repeat the course a few times.
7. Now add something to step *into* at the beginning of the course. Large stainless steel mixing bowls work well, as do cardboard boxes or frying pans.

8. Demonstrate, then let your toddler repeat it on her own.

Suggestions: Keep it simple, and keep it visual. Adding things like clapping hands or touching the ground may be too hard to remember, but when she sees the chair it will help her remember what to do.

It's better to make it too easy than too hard, and you can always add on as your toddler becomes more competent.

"Obstacle Course" is great outdoors because there's more room, but it's also a lifesaver on rainy days.

Variations: Instead of adding more new sections to the course, repeat a favorite one. Even alternating between two things (stool and towels, for example) can be fun.

Let older children add their own ideas to the course. If that makes it too difficult for your toddler, have them arrange their own course!

66
Countdown

Origin: Everyone was quite proud of Katie when she learned to count, somewhat erratically, to ten. But beyond getting a rise out of everyone, Katie really didn't understand the concept behind her recital. So we played "Countdown."

Equipment: Something to count—blocks, spoons, raisins, or fingers—any group of similar objects.

Position: You can sit at a table or on the floor. Pile the objects to be counted next to you.

Procedure:
1. Put two blocks out in front of your toddler. (For some reason it was easier for Katie to start with two than with one!)
2. Ask, "How many blocks are there?"
3. She may answer correctly, or she may, like Katie, rush through several numbers. "One, two, three, five . . . eight!"

4. Regardless of her response, take her hand and count with her as she touches each block. Say "one" as her hand touches the first block and "two" as she touches the second.

5. Sum up. "Two! There are two blocks here."

6. Add a block, and ask again, "Now how many blocks are there?"

7. Again, touch her hand to each block as you count together. "One, two, three! Now there are three blocks!"

8. Add a fourth block, and repeat steps 5 and 6.

9. Let her count the four blocks by herself, but encourage her to touch each block as she counts.

10. You can now work backwards, removing the blocks one at a time.

Suggestions: We only went up to four, maybe five, for a long time. It was one thing to recite one through ten, but quite another to actually count that many objects!

Because they are used to reciting numbers, toddlers often count too fast, counting four when there are only three objects. If you teach her only to count as she touches an object, it will help slow her down.

Variations: By removing all the blocks, you can introduce the concept of zero.

Older kids will enjoy not only counting to higher numbers but also counting backwards as you remove blocks.

67
Jack-in-the-Box

Origin: Katie learned this game in our "Mommy and Me" tots tumbling class with instructor Peggy Shima. It quickly became a favorite.

Equipment: None.

Position: Sit with your toddler on the floor.

Procedure:
1. Ask, "Would you like to learn a jack-in-the-box game?"
2. Continue, "Okay, you be the jack-in-the-box. Crouch down and hide yourself!" Help her tuck into a hiding crouch.
3. Then say, "Jack-in-the-box
   Lies oh so still.
   Will she come out?
   Yes, she will!"
4. And on "Yes, she will!" pick your toddler up around the waist and lift her into the air.
5. It's not likely she'll be satisfied with just one turn, so repeat a few times,

Jack-in-the-Box

always making sure the "Yes, she will!" is a dramatic finish.

Variations: You can let your toddler spring up on her own when she hears her cue, or your jack-in-the-box can crouch behind a chair and jump out to surprise you at just the right moment. We had a problem with Katie, however, who refused to spring out, and we'd have to call again, "Ahem. Yes, she will! Oh, jack-in-the-box, it's time to spring out!" But she'd just giggle until we finally reached around and sprang her up and over the chair.

Cover your toddler with a towel, and on "Yes, she will!" she leaps out from under her cover.

68

Color Code

Origin: The first color Katie learned to identify was yellow. When asked "What color is this?" of a nonyellow item, Katie would respond, "Not yellow!" We played "Color Code" so she could learn the other primary colors.

Equipment: Building blocks, stringing beads, or stacking cups in primary colors.

Position: Any.

Procedure: 1. Pour the blocks into a pile on the floor or table.
2. Say, "Look at all these blocks! All different colors. What color do you like?"
3. Have her select a block and repeat its color after you. "Yellow. You have a yellow block."
4. Now suggest, "Let's put all the yellow blocks together."
5. Help her sort the yellow blocks into

233

their own pile, saying, "Here's a yellow block! Can you find a block that is the same as this yellow one?"

6. Once all the yellow blocks are together, choose another color to sort out. "Now let's find all the blue blocks."

7. Show her a blue block, and say, "Here is a blue block. Can you find a block that is the same blue color as this one?"

8. Continue sorting the remaining blocks into their color-coded piles.

9. Mix the blocks together and start over.

Suggestions: Let your toddler take her time. She may have to keep checking the color in question in her search for the right color.

"Color Code" also teaches the concepts of *same* and *different*. It may be easier for your toddler to find a block of the same color than to find a yellow or blue block. This is a good start to identifying colors as she is still having to differentiate between them.

Variations: Cut strips of colored paper, put them in an envelope, and play "Color Code" in a restaurant or car.

For older children, use a wider variety of colors. They can sort crayons into shades of yellow, brown, purple, and so on.

69
Tea Time

Origin: When Katie was into pouring from one container into another, we moved our play tea set from inside to outside. This way she could have the fun of serving "tea" in tiny plastic cups, and I could relax and enjoy the "party."

Equipment: A plastic toy tea set.

Position: See below.

Procedure:

1. Help your toddler arrange her tea set on an outside patio table, cement porch, or backyard lawn.
2. Help her fill the tea pot or pitcher with water.
3. Then, falling into the role of invited guest, say, "Oh, hello! May I please have some tea?" Be sure to use a sickly sweet voice—she'll love it!
4. Let her serve you your drink (hold your cup steady, though), pouring all by herself. That's why you're outside, remember!

5. Take a sip and exclaim, "Oh, it's delicious!" or "Oh! Too hot! I'll have to let it cool," or even "Yuck! There's a bug in my tea!" Any dramatic reaction will do.

6. Drink it down if you dare, or discreetly pour it out behind your back (another good reason to be outside!).

7. Now you're ready for a refill. "May I have another cup, please?"

8. And suggest that she fill up other cups for any imaginary guests who might be dropping by.

9. Continue your charade of too hot, too cold, too spicy, or just right until your little hostess is "poured out."

Suggestions: Be sure to ham it up, because it's your reaction that will give "Tea Time" a comical flair. You can even fake a spill. It's fun for your toddler to have the shoe on the other foot.

Variations: Turn the hose on to a trickle, set out a variety of containers (measuring cups, buckets, bowls, and so on), and your toddler will be happy to play independently for quite some time.

Amy quickly became bored with plain old water, so we put a few drops of food coloring into her bowls and plastic cups. You should have seen her face!

70
Your House or Mine?

Origin: When Amy was four she received a cardboard Mickey Mouse playhouse for her birthday. Then Katie, of course, needed a house of her own. Hence, the classic card table and blanket house.

Equipment: Card table and several blankets (one never seems to be quite enough). You can use the dining room or kitchen table, but a card table is nice because it can be set up in a relatively out-of-the-way place. A flashlight adds a nice touch.

Position: See below.

Procedure: 1. Ask your toddler, "How would you like to have your very own house?" She'll look a little surprised. Continue, "All we need is a table and some blankets."

2. As you set up her house, explain, "The table will be your roof, and the blankets make walls. See?"

239

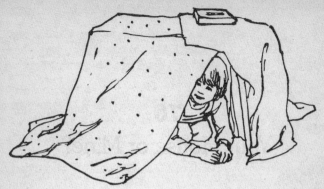

Your House or Mine?

3. Leave an opening for a door.
4. If your toddler is reluctant to go in, you go first, and then call to her, "Come on in! It's a great house!"
5. Sit inside the house for a few minutes discussing how cozy it is and perhaps where the kitchen is or the back door.
6. If you have a flashlight handy, suggest, "What your house needs is a little light!" Show her how to turn it on and off.
7. Explain that you must go back now to your house but that you'll be back to visit a little later.
8. Or suggest that she come visit you in a few minutes.
9. Spend some time going back and forth between houses (yours being wherever you happen to be at the time). Discuss the traffic on the way

over, road conditions ("quite icy coming over the bridge"), and what errands need to be done that day.

Suggestions: If she doesn't think of it, suggest that she select some books, dolls, or toys to make her house more livable!

You can invest in a small plastic tent or cardboard house like we did, but, to tell the truth, all children will agree that tables and blankets, pillows, and couches make better houses!

Variations: When Amy played, the Mickey Mouse clubhouse was everything from a hospital to a library.

71
Buried Alive!

Origin: Pillows, being soft and light, make for great games. This one came about when a stack of them fell on Katie during another game.

Equipment: Lots of pillows or soft cushions.

Position: Sit on the floor or couch with your toddler. Have pillows nearby.

Procedure:
1. Suggest, "Let's play with all these pillows. How would you like to be buried alive?" And "buried alive" should be said rather dramatically. She probably won't know what it means, but it will sound exciting!
2. Have your toddler stretch out on the couch.
3. Starting at her feet, slowly cover her up with the pillows.
4. Say, "There go the feet, buried alive. There go the legs, buried alive."
5. As soon as she's all covered up, say,

"Oh! What happened to Katie? Where is she?"

6. If your toddler doesn't burst out at this point, then remove the pillows one at a time.

7. As you uncover various body parts, exclaim, "Aha! Here's a leg," or "What's this hand doing in my pillows?"

8. After she's completely revealed, start all over.

Suggestions: Your toddler may not want her head buried, so just play "Buried Alive!" from the neck down.

Variations: Instead of taking the pillows off her, tunnel your way in to where she's hiding.

Or, once she's buried alive, pretend to sit on her, saying, "Oh, look at this nice

Buried Alive!

pile of pillows. I think I'll just rest here a moment." Sit only on the lower body area, though.

Before we discovered "Buried Alive!" we were playing a game in which we'd pile all the pillows up in a big tower and Katie would leap into them.

72
Fun in a Swing

Origin: Quite by accident, Katie bumped into me while swinging. It got a laugh, and "Fun in a Swing" was born.

Equipment: A swing.

Position: Stand facing your toddler, who is in the swing.

Procedure:
1. Standing in front of your toddler, give her a few pushes against her knees to get her going.
2. Then, turn your back to her and say, "Oh, I'd better be going now."
3. Only pretend to walk away. With your back to your toddler, allow her swing to come up behind you and bump you in the back.
4. Feigning surprise, say, "Hey! Cut that out! You bumped into me!"
5. By now, she'll be heading back in your direction. Again, allow the swing to bump you.

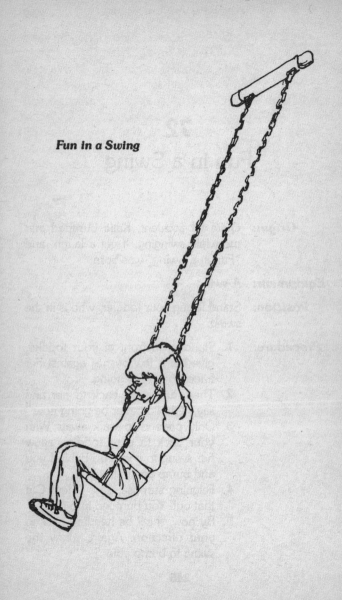

Fun in a Swing

6. Act surprised. "Hey, I thought I told you to cut that out!"

7. Continue along this line a few more times.

8. Now, catch her swing in midair as it comes toward you. Say, "Now listen here, I *said* to leave me alone!"

9. Push her away, and pretend to walk away, only to be bumped into again!

10. Katie could have played this all day. If you tire of the game, as we did, give her fair warning before you stop.

Suggestions: Don't push your toddler too high in the swing, or you may get bumped harder than you'd planned. Katie used to laugh so hard we were afraid she'd fall right out of the swing!

Variations: There are as many games to play in a swing as there are children swinging, but we found that a quick tickle every time she came our way was always good for a laugh, as was a gentle poke in the tummy.

"Underdoggies" were also family favorites. I don't know why, but it is what we called them when I was a child. Stand behind your toddler in her swing. Holding the sides of the swing seat, push the swing out in front of you as you run forward until you go completely under your toddler and come out in front of her. Most children adore the thrill of an "underdoggie," but this should only be done with young toddlers in swings with safety straps.

73

Sort the Silver

Origin: Without recognizing the educational benefits, I assigned Katie the job of putting the silver into its case just to give her something to do.

Equipment: A case in which silverware is kept or the plastic container for your everyday stainless steel. Forks and spoons of all sizes.

Position: Dump out all the silverware, and place the empty case or holder beside it. Remove the knives if it makes you feel more comfortable.

Procedure: 1. Demonstrate where the spoons go, as opposed to the forks and knives.
2. Do the same for the forks.
3. Now suggest, "Can you put all these spoons and forks away? The spoons go here, and the forks go here!"
4. Watch her to see if she understood.
5. Praise her the first few times she sorts them correctly.

Sort the Silver

6. When she's done, dump them out and start over.

Suggestions: If you've got soup or iced tea spoons, add them to the game. The same goes for salad forks.

Variations: If you haven't got a silverware case or holder (or you'd rather not use it), trace the spoons and forks onto a piece of paper, and have your toddler sort them on that.

Let your toddler sort other kitchen utensils by size, color, or shape. Even mixing bowls can be arranged small, medium, and large.

74
Log Rolls

Origin: This is a game that Katie's cousin, Ryan, and his mom taught us.

Equipment: None.

Position: Lie on your back with your toddler on top of you, tummy to tummy.

Procedure:
1. Say, "Hang on to my neck! We're going to do some log rolls!"
2. Wrap your arms around her middle.
3. Now roll to the right. Say, "Log roll this way."
4. Then roll to the left and continue, "Log roll this way!"
5. Continue back and forth several times, each time tipping your toddler further and further over.
6. Now roll all the way over, supporting your weight by your arms so as not to flatten your toddler. Say, "Oh! We log rolled all the way over!"
7. Check her reaction.

Log Rolls

8. If she enjoyed the full roll, repeat steps 3 through 6; if the full roll worried her, only go through step 5.

Suggestions: You might want to eliminate shoes and belts for this one.

Variations: Ryan used to say "squish squash, squish squash" as they rocked back and forth, but "tick tock" or "flip flop" would work too.

Try "Log Rolls" in a grassy area outside. We used to log roll down a grassy hill and soon learned how the game got its name!

75
Warm-Ups

Origin: Just try to work through Jane Fonda or any other exercise tape or show without your toddler joining in!

Equipment: Music.

Position: Stand facing each other.

Procedure:

1. Put on a record or tape of music familiar to her.
2. Begin with a simple stretch, saying, "Reach up to the ceiling."
3. Put one hand on your hip and curve the other one over your head, leaning to the side. Count, "One, two, three, four."
4. Switch hands and count again.
5. Straddle your legs and go down for some toe touches.
6. Count to four again.
7. Sit on the floor in a straddle position.
8. With the opposite arm, stretch down to your toes. Ask, "Can you

touch your nose to your knees?"
(She probably can!)

9. Try raising and lowering your legs
while lying flat on your back. "Up,
two, three, four. Down, two, three,
four."

10. Had enough?

Suggestions: Don't attempt an official exercise tape; it
would be too difficult for your toddler to
follow. There are, however, some exercise records for children, such as
"Mousercise" with Mickey Mouse, and
even Strawberry Shortcake has her own
exercise routine!

Variations: Any exercise you do, let your toddler
try. She will modify it to suit her abilities,
and it certainly can't do any harm.